Too Serious a Business

DONALD CAMERON WATT

TOO
SERIOUS
A
BUSINESS

European armed forces and the approach to the Second World War

UNIVERSITY OF CALIFORNIA PRESS
Berkeley and Los Angeles · 1975

UNIVERSITY OF CALIFORNIA PRESS
Berkeley and Los Angeles, California

ISBN: 0-520-02829-5
Library of Congress Catalog Card
Number: 74-82853
Dec. 2, 1975

Printed in Great Britain

*This book is based on the Lees Knowles Lectures
delivered at Cambridge University during the
winter of 1973 by D. C. Watt, Professor of
International History in the University of London*

Contents

for Felicia

War is too serious a business to be left to soldiers.

GEORGES CLEMENCEAU

Preface

These lectures were given in Cambridge in the Michaelmas term of 1973. They are essentially an attempt at a synthesis of other men's work, although I have called on my own research, and that of others, into the primary materials whenever I could. Being a work of synthesis, some of its undoubted defects spring from the gaps in the monograph literature which are large and peculiar. There is, for example, little or nothing on the social position and role of the British officer class. There is no work that focuses on the political role of the General Staff in Britain. Much remains to be done on the development of military doctrine in France and on the role of the General Staff under General Gamelin. More surprisingly, there is, at the moment of writing, no satisfactory study of the evolution of the doctrine of the *armoured Blitzkrieg* in Germany. And, apart from the work of M. Rochat, academic study of the Italian armed forces has hardly begun.

The invitation to deliver these lectures came from the Master and Fellows of Trinity College, Cambridge, to whose kindness and hospitality I owe much. To G. Kitson Clark, the *fons et origo* of the invitation and my unfailingly courteous host on my six weekly visits to Cambridge I have to pay an especial tribute. For help in access to the collections at Churchill College, Cambridge, my thanks are due to Captain Stephen Roskill and to Miss Angela Raspin, the archivist. My work on the German naval and military archives has, over the years, been greatly assisted by the librarian of the Foreign and Commonwealth Office, the Enemy Documents Section of the Admiralty, the Historical Section of the United States Office of the Navy, the Library of Congress, the librarian of St Anthony's College, Oxford, the Rockefeller Foundation (who financed my visit to Washington in 1960–61) and the Central Research Fund of the University of London (which generously financed my purchases of microfilm of German army records).

Over the years I have learnt enormously from Captain Roskill and Professor Michael Howard. I have benefited from the courteous help of Professor Norman Gibbs of Oxford. My thanks are also due to my students, past and present, whose original research has so greatly helped me, especially Professor Laurence Pratt of the University of Alberta, Professor Robert Young of the University of Winnipeg and Mr Uri Bialer of the Hebrew University of Jerusalem. I have benefited, too, from the aid and advice of the official historians in France, of Mr Clifton Child of the Historical Section of the Cabinet Office and of my colleagues on the British Committee for the History of the Second World War. None of these, however, need take any responsibility for the views expressed in these pages.

April 1974

D. C. WATT

1 The Nature of the European Civil War, 1919-1939

The theme of this book is the role of European armed forces and the approach of the Second World War. Its origins arise in a remark made several years ago on the contrast between this role and that played by their predecessors in the events leading up to the outbreak of the First World War. In 1914 a belligerent military urged a reluctant civilian leadership into war, even to the extent of using deceit and misrepresentations to secure the vital orders from the Kaiser, the Austrian Emperor and the Czar. In 1938-9 the reverse was the case. It was the military leadership, whatever its nationality, which dragged its feet. The British Chiefs of Staff provided pessimistic prophecies of defeat until well after Munich. General Beck resigned the position of Chief of Staff of the German army rather than see his country once again plunge down the road to disaster. His successors organised a military conspiracy which lost its *raison d'être* when Chamberlain went to Munich. General Pariani, Chief of the Italian Army Staff, provided the gloomiest prognostications of defeat to all who would listen. General Vuillemin of the French air force, gulled and swindled by a series of Potemkin villages—or rather, airfields—returned from Germany in 1938 convinced that war would mean the ruin of Paris. The driving force towards war came from the civilians not the military.

The argument in these chapters is that the Second World War was, in origin and for at least its first twenty-one months,

a civil war confined to Europe. Russia, although there is much
to be said about its armed forces, had by 1939 ceased to be part
of Europe in any real sense of the word. In his rise to power
Stalin had caused the division and delivery for destruction of
much of the European revolutionary socialist movement. The
bulk of the surviving emigré leadership of this movement was
an almost incidental casualty in the great purges. These fell
equally harshly on a Soviet High Command trained in co-
operation with the *Reichswehr*, and on Leningrad, the most
European of Russia's cities, deliberately built by Peter the Great
to be Russia's window on to Europe. The purges broke much
of the extraordinary European Comintern organisation headed
by Willi Münzenberg, himself murdered in strange circumstances during the fall of France. The most militant of the
rank and file of the European revolutionary movement fell in
the Spanish Civil War, or were handed over from French
internment to the Gestapo in 1940, as were those of the
German Communist leadership whom Stalin could not break
to his will. The Nazi–Soviet pact and Soviet action against
Poland, Finland, the Baltic states and Bessarabia completed the
picture of a Soviet Union withdrawing from an entity with
which its only relations were to be those of war and conquest.

The Second World War ended the hegemony of the powers
of western and central Europe. In its place now stands the
hegemony of the extra-European powers, dragged from their
isolation in 1941. Until 1941, the war, with its fifty million
deaths, its starvation, disruption, destruction and chaos, the
wilful physical destruction (by those whom Arnold Toynbee
would call the barbarians within the gates) of much of Europe's
heritage of art and architecture, was a war of purely European
dimensions, the battlefields confined to the areas west of longti-
tude 25° east.

For most of its first two years, the Second World War was

largely confined to Europe and to Europe's approaches. But it
was more than simply an extension of what Mr A. J. P. Taylor
has called 'the struggle for mastery in Europe'. To very many
people who lived through the years of the 1930s, what seemed
to be in train was not the approach of another war between
states, but the preliminary stages of a civil war taking place
throughout Europe. The shelling of the Karl Marx Hof in
Vienna in 1934, the movement of Italian armies and
British warships through the Mediterranean in the autumn of
1935, the bombs falling on Madrid, on Barcelona and on
Guernica in 1936 and 1937, the rumble of German armour
across the Austrian borders and into the Sudeten foothills in
1938, seemed to them all to be parts of a process embracing all
Europe, a civil war between the forces of oligarchy, aristocracy,
authoritarianism, Fascism and those of popular democracy,
socialism, revolution. The British governments of the day could
not be forgiven their failure to condemn the forces of the right.
Since they did not condemn, they were taken to approve. And
a whole school of political comment sprang up, seeking a socio-
economic and political rationale for that assumed approval.
Since 1945 few but a handful of the young, a scattering of
Americans, radicals and Anglophobes, some survivors of the
1930s and the historians of the Soviet bloc can be found to
repeat that particular line of argument. Attention has focused
instead on the national grounds for the policies followed by the
British government, on the disparity between Britain's mani-
fold military and financial weaknesses and the parallel threats
to her interests in peace in Western Europe, in the Mediterranean and Middle East, and in the Far East. The massive
release of the British records under the Public Records Act of
1967 has swamped and obliterated the last of those who sought
to explain British policy in terms of ideological affinities. And
the civil war theory has been lost sight of in the ensuing flood

of detailed monographs, past, present and undoubtedly to come.

Not for the first time, historiographical fashion has emptied the baby out with the bathwater. Historians ignore at their peril the beliefs and attitudes of contemporary witnesses to the events they are studying. If contemporaries spoke of a European civil war, their image of Europe, their perception of common elements in the course of events in the various countries of Europe are themselves evidence worthy of study, even where those perceptions were formed only on the basis of the public face of events and in ignorance of all those aspects which escaped general attention at the time. In some sense, then, contemporary witnesses felt the existence of a common European political society, a *civitas Europae* and identified those elements in it which were in conflict with each other. The outbreak of war in 1939 marked the failure to conserve or maintain any part of this common society, a failure which had become apparent much earlier with the rise of Fascism and Nazism and their rejection of most of the conventions which had hitherto governed national behaviour within this society. September 1939 seemed to mark the return of the European states to a condition of Hobbesian nature. But when, in the summer of 1940, the France of the Third Republic succumbed to military defeat and sued for armistice, when the Assemblée Nationale abandoned its powers to the aged Marshal Pétain and a military dictatorship based on Vichy, this was felt to be a disaster on a European rather than on a purely national scale. Apart from a scattering of pusillanimous, if not fellow travelling neutrals, Britain alone remained as a home for Europe's exiles and the last hope of a restoration of democracy in Europe.

Clearly, there were elements of civil conflict within most of the major states of Europe before 1939. Within the democracies they were often localised: the Paris riots of February

1934, the occupation of factories during the early days of the Popular Front, the conspiracy of the Cagoulards, the street battles in the East End between Mosley's supporters, the police and the local inhabitants, for example. In those states which had succumbed to totalitarian rule, the battles had come earlier; in Italy in 1920–22; in Germany in the Ruhr and lower Saxony in 1923 and in the street battles in Berlin in 1931–2. By 1939 the defeated were marked out for the concentration camp. But their defeat was only temporary.

In all the major powers the same phenomena can be observed between the wars: political groups wearing uniform, acknowledging a commander or leader, organised on quasi-military lines, using violence against their political opponents; a party, preaching violent social and political revolution, pledging the loyalty of its members to and subject to directions from the Soviet authorities rather than to those of its own state; street-violence; anti-semitism. These are, however, not enough in themselves to be classified as European phenomena characteristic of a European society as such, rather than as particular to the individual national societies in which they occurred. What made them European was their common origin and their interconnections and interactions.

By the mid 1930s these phenomena had produced in most countries of Europe a dissolution of the normal social and political processes into civil disorder or civil strife. They all have their origin in the years before 1914 which saw the breakdown of the European states system. They were strengthened and accentuated by the wartime strains of privation, siege, enormous battlefield casualties, and the deaths caused by flu or starvation in the nine months between Armistice and Peace Treaty. The botched job done at the Paris peace conference of replacing and repairing the links which had held Europe together only reinforced them.

Before 1914 Europe was clearly a 'transnational society' in Raymond Aron's coinage.[1] The social and political links which bound its governments and peoples together were to prove weaker in July 1914 than those which briefly buried the domestic discords of the belligerents in the *Burgfrieden* or the *Union Sacrée*. But despite their failure in 1914, these links had been strong enough over the previous century to keep Europe from dissolution through the processes of German and Italian unifications, the withdrawal of the Ottoman empire in Europe, the scramble for Africa, the plunder of China.

One can identify five separate sets of these links. Firstly, the states of Europe related in their political concerns, in their fears of war and hope of assistance more to each other than to the non-European world. They formed a political system. Secondly, to avoid gratuitous conflict, their statesmen and diplomatists had evolved a set of rules and conventions amounting almost to customary law to govern their relations with each other, which, if often broken, were still sufficiently widely accepted for the breaches to be recognised as such. They had, in addition, developed institutions of co-operation such as the ambassadors' conference, the statesmen's congress, the investment banks consortia, etc. Thirdly, the ruling classes, the nobility and the *haute bourgeoisie*, intermingled socially, travelling in one another's countries, taking the waters in Baden Baden or shooting grouse in Badenoch together, and intermarried. The leaders of the professional classes, whose social importance was rising less rapidly than their value to the societies they served, entered increasingly into international scientific, academic and social association.[2] Fourthly, it was widely assumed that the inhabitants of this European society shared a common intellectual and cultural heritage from classical Greece and Rome, enriched by its passage through the art and literature of the Italian Renaissance; within this heritage English literature, painting

and design mingled with and enriched the art and literature
of Paris and Vienna which, in their turn, fed on the music and
the philosophy of German university towns and of the courts of
Hapsburg Vienna. Exotic importations such as Moroccan
decoration, Russian ballet, Chinese and Japanese painting and
ceramics were to some extent shared by all.

At their upper levels, the states of Europe related to each
other's military, financial and industrial might, acknowledged
common conventions, mingled their own ruling classes together, partook of a common culture, even, up to a certain
point, shared a common morality. It was a Europe for Harrods'
customers, not for those of Woolworths, it is true. One of the
more difficult questions to answer is how it catered for the
customers of the Army and Navy or the Civil Service Stores.

One can, perhaps, answer this question by looking more
closely at the position occupied and the part played by the
armed services in the various national societies and at the effects
of the war of 1914-18 and its aftermath upon that position.
To do this in detail will be the task of a later chapter. Here
one only need note that in the main European monarchies the
officer corps of the armed forces provided the support on which
in their traditionalist-deferential societies even the monarchies
themselves rested. They were tied intimately into the land-
owning nobility. And the hierarchical societies bound them
into the order on which they rested by professional, personal
and class loyalties, and by the convention (which now survives
only in the United States of America) that the business of
government fell into two rigidly separated spheres, the civil
and the military. Each of these had its own head—the
Chancellor and the Chief of Staff—the ultimate responsible
advisers to the unifying factor, the head of state, who was also
head of government and Commander-in-Chief. The officer
corps in general, the officers of the élite units more particularly,

and the staff corps from which alone positions of real seniority could be reached most especially, were the ultimate defenders of the *status quo*, bound to the state by their personal oaths of loyalty to its head. Order, authority, autocracy, tradition were the qualities which they were dedicated to preserving. Even in France, where no head of state of monarchical status existed to focus the loyalties of the officer corps, its members were tied by their residual monarchism, and by their Catholicism, to the party of order and to an idealised France, the *pays réelle* as opposed to the *pays légale*. Their defeat at the hands of Captain Dreyfus's protagonists was to combine with this metaphysical solution to their problems of loyalty and identification, to form the first stage towards the tragic but vulgar farce of Vichy. As nationally-oriented as they were, the officer corps only partook through their membership of the European aristocracy in the social relationships which made of pre-war Europe something more than a geographical expression. They did, however, play an extremely important part in the power relationships which made Europe a political system.

These relationships, the position of the states of Europe towards and in relation to one another, rested in fact fairly and squarely on the size, efficacy and efficiency of their armed forces. Military or naval power was one of the four essential elements of national strength. The European system of states and the systems of government which survived in them in 1914 were, to a considerable extent, the product of five hundred years of internecine war. They had survived, in fact, because of the efficiency with which they waged war, and because of their organisation as war-waging bodies. By comparison with the states and empires of the non-European world, their organisation for war made them superior long before European technology had provided them with the edge they enjoyed at the end of the nineteenth century. The armed forces themselves depended on a system of loyalty and discipline within the community at large which gave its members that singleness of mind and mutual confidence which is the basis of high morale, whether its content is religious or nationalistic or racial. They could not have functioned without an efficient and comparatively uncorrupt administration, capable of seeing that their members were efficiently led, clothed and armed. The food, clothes and arms in turn could not have been provided, if there were not the finances to pay for them, finances available not merely in specie but in taxable capacity, trade and above all the paper-credit necessary for prolonged war. No non-European state had evolved comparable institutions. The drawbacks of the system were experienced in Prussia and France at the end of the eighteenth century. The demands of the armed forces for large numbers of rank and file necessitated a large officer corps, which could only come from the nobility. The consequent necessity of preserving the privileges of the nobility prevented any alliance between monarch and bourgeois, tied the nobility firmly to the monarchy and made of the officer corps a body rigidly identified with and pledged to defend the social and political *status quo*.

At the head of the armed forces stood the body responsible for military advice to the political leadership of the nation and for the command of the armed forces in war. The standing of its country in relation to other countries and even its survival depended on the manner in which it fulfilled this responsibility. War, it used to be said, was the ultimate reason of kings, the final touchstone. If we are to discuss the role of the armed forces of the major European powers in the events leading up to the outbreak of the Second World War, it is on the commanders and advisers that our attention must initially be focused. The contention that both within the major powers Germany, France, Italy, Britain, Poland and the Soviet Union,

and in the conflict which engulfed them there was a measure
of civil strife necessitates our examining them under four
different heads, to which the following four chapters are
devoted.

In the first place there is the role which the commanders and
advisers, the General Staff in fact, played in relation to their
own political societies. To what extent did they identify with
them? How far were their loyalties engaged to the survival of
the political system they served? How far did they stand apart
from the political system they served? And how far did the
divided society of their particular country have confidence in
their loyalties and efficiency?

The second factor is the degree of effectiveness which the
members of the General Staff exhibit as a military, war-winning
element. The twentieth century was a time of very rapid technological change. The development of the tank, the machine-
gun, the submarine, the bombing aircraft, radio and radar
made the war of 1939–45 considerably different in character
from that of 1914–18. The effectiveness of national armed
forces in the defence of their respective states and in the pursuit
of the respective governments' political objectives depends on
the degree to which the commanders and advisers can adapt
and refine the manner in which they conduct war and the
view of warfare which inspires the arming and training of their
troops, to the changing technologies and circumstances of war.
Too little adaptation and they may find themselves faced with
techniques of warfare to which they have no more answers than
the Zulus, that nation pre-eminently organised for war, had to
the Maxim guns which destroyed them at Ulundi. Too rapid
a rate of experimentation and they may find themselves, like
the French Air Force in 1938, with a multitude of prototypes
but no mass supply. Too early a transition from development
to production and the army reaches a technological peak which

others, starting later, may easily overtake. In 1934 the
Air Force was the most advanced in the world. N
Balbo's bombing planes could outstrip the fighter airc̶̶̶̶ ̶̶
every other air force. But in 1940 much of the Italian Air
Force was obsolete. If Britain had fought in September 1938
she could well have been forced to fight the battle of Britain
with one squadron of Hurricanes, one Spitfire and a radar
chain untested and incomplete, whereas in 1940 both aircraft
and aircraft location devices had been tried in practice and
brought to battlefield readiness.

The third factor we have to consider is the range of strategic
postures taken by the powers of Europe towards each other.
What kind of war and against what enemies did the commanders and advisers of the respective powers expect to have
to fight? What kind of attack did they fear? Did this strategic
doctrine turn on defence or offence? And how did they see their
potential enemies? What estimate did they form of their
ability to make war? How good were their intelligence-
gathering machines? What philosophy of war governed the
assessments made of the evidence they gathered? How had
their strategic doctrines evolved since the war of 1914-18?

When and if we elucidate the answers to these questions, we
can turn to the fourth and, for this book, most important set
of questions for any consideration of the role of European
armed forces in the approach of the Second World War, questions which all stem from one initial enquiry. Given the kind
of enemy they expected, given the kind of war they expected and
trained themselves to fight, given that by 1937 or so the
imminent peril of a second European war was something to
which they all had to reconcile themselves, what did the commanders and advisers actually do? What advice did they give
their governments? What part did they, in fact, play in the
events which led up to the German attack on Poland and the

subsequent disaster of the French defeat and the expulsion of British forces from the Continent?

The final set of questions we have to answer is posed not so much by the theme of this book but by the answers it provides. That phase of the Second World War which was confined to the European powers ended in 1941 with the German attack on Russia and the Japanese assault on Pearl Harbor. The Italian armed forces sued for armistice in 1943. By 1945 units of the new Italian state were fighting against their former allies. A new French army had been built by the French in exile, an army whose tragic experiences in the wars of decolonisation were to lead to a new crisis and a new Republic in 1958. The German army, or a section of it, tried and failed to destroy its political master on 20 July 1944. Thereafter it fought to the bitter end. New German armies were to be raised in a divided Europe some six or more years later. How did the armed forces conduct themselves in the final disintegration of Europe? What lessons did they derive from it? And what advice did their commanders give as military advisers to the dwarfed and dwindled European power system which emerged at the end of the war?

There are still other points: the question of how far the Harrods-style Europe of the first decade of the twentieth century survived into the post–1918 period; how far it is legitimate to speak of a disruption of European society between the wars; in what ways that disruption was manifested, and what new factors, if any, entered into this hypothetical process.

Inevitably, one has to begin with a few clichés. At the political level it was intended by the peace-makers after the First World War that there should be a universal political system to maintain peace and security, the League of Nations. The circumstances of the League's creation in a peace conference devoted to the settlement of a war, all of whose major battlefields had lain in Europe, already gave it a markedly European rationale. The exclusion of the United States and the Soviet Union from the League, even though both powers moved into closer association with Europe at the end of the 1920s through the mechanism of the Preparatory Commission to the Disarmament Conference, and although the Soviet Union actually joined the League in 1934, gave its membership, its deliberations, its ethos, an essentially European character and preoccupations. The League suffered, however, from its attempts to substitute juristical formalism for the rules and conventions which had evolved to govern the power relationships of the European great powers in the nineteenth century. Moreover, since the elements in this formalism were specifically inspired by the notion that they could be substituted for these power relationships, which would then in some way cease to be, they in no sense corresponded with them. They failed, therefore, to sustain the confidence placed in them once they came up against the realities of power relationships, as they did over Manchuria and Abyssinia. When formal law ceases to be enforceable, confidence in it disappears—hence the frantic rush into collective neutrality by Belgium and the small states signatory to the Copenhagen Declaration of 1938,[3] just as its more deep-rooted conventions were to disappear under the anarchy of Hitler's attitude to international politics. This anarchy was expressed in his willingness to destroy states as such. And naked power relationships were not enough to restrain a Hitler whose miscalculations increased the more he tried to manipulate events to his purpose rather than to wait on them. The war that began in September 1939 was the outcome.

It is to these actual power relationships that this book is really directed. Armed forces, it was said, played an essential part in them before 1914 by their size in relation to each other, by their role in holding domestic society together and preserving internal order, hierarchy, discipline and morale, by their embodiment and perpetuation of national tradition and national selfconsciousness. In stable societies the armed forces rested on and maintained stability. But what happened if the societies to which they belonged and the governments they served were no longer stable? The role of the army leadership in an unstable society might be expected to influence its pattern of behaviour, even including in this the advice it gave to its political masters. And with changes in the social composition of the political leadership it served, changes in its own social composition, and in its degree of identification with the society it served might also prove of importance.

It has been suggested that pre-1914 Europe partook of the nature of a society in five respects: the power relationships between its states; the rules and conventions which governed their behaviour one to another; the social relationships between their élites; the shared culture; and the common moralities of largely Christian states and peoples.

At the end of the 1914-18 war the first of these was inevitably altered by the following factors: the defeat of Germany, the disappearance of Austria–Hungary, the reappearance of the Polish state, the exclusion of Soviet Russia after the defeat of the Red Army before Warsaw, and the substitution for the Hapsburg–Russian confrontation across the corpse of the Ottoman Empire in Europe, of a *macedoine* of inter-Balkan imperialisms over such issues as Macedonia, the Dobrudja, Transylvania, the Banat, Fiume. The underlying economics and actuarial realities however left Germany potentially by far the most powerful state in central Europe. European politics became dominated by the issue of revisionism, revision, that is, of the *status quo* established at Versailles.

Of the remaining four points, the efforts of the League of

Nations to provide new rules and conventions has already been noted. Its potentialities for keeping the peace rested on the assumption that aggression would be immediately obvious as the abnormality it was considered to be and that all members of the League would come together to end it. The non-European character of the Soviet Union can be seen in the underlying assumption of the Soviet security system, a network of bilateral non-aggression pacts with neighbours, the underlying assumption of which was that war was the normal state of relations between the Soviet state and its non-Soviet neighbours and that formal undertakings were necessary to avoid this governing Soviet relations with those states in a position to attack her or to act as a base for such attacks.[4]

As to the other three points, very great differences can be observed after the 1914–18 war. Since the position of the social élites that had ruled the major European powers before 1914, was largely destroyed or broken by the revolutions, the inflations and the social changes of the war and post-war years, their links with similar groups in other countries lost any political importance. Pre-war society dwindled to the publicity-seeking self-indulgence of the café, the casino and the illustrated papers. The common culture continued though the divisions between Paris and Central Europe were accentuated, and the creative élites of Europe drew further and further apart from those societies which gave them birth. Much of modern art, music, theatre, even literature and architecture, was self-consciously anti-bourgeois and intent on developing new forms of expression unacceptable, even unrecognisable as such to all but an extremely limited number of the very wealthy and very educated. The role of a common culture in holding European political society together was greatly diminished. Equally significantly, much of the creative work of the pre-war period fell victim to the propaganda of the war, so that, to this day,

Nietzsche and Wagner can still be used as stereotypes of barbarism. It is only in recent years that the German and Austrian painters of the *Sezession,* of *die Brücke* or the *Blaue Reiter* movements, apart from the Swiss Paul Klee, have achieved any real recognition west of the Rhine. To some extent the centripetal role of the pre-war aristocracy was taken over by professional associations based on education and science (as, for example, the German Rhodes Scholars or the nuclear scientists sitting at Lord Rutherford's feet), on finance, especially after the foundation of the Bank of International Settlements in 1928, or on diplomacy. The regular meetings of the League Council and Assembly and the multiplicity of other conferences were to create friendships across the national boundaries that can be seen in operation in the dark days of the 1930s. Much more important, however, are the links of ideology, the internationals, communist and anti-communist, fascist and anti-fascist, conservative catholic and conservative protestant. Their importance was enhanced by the degree to which the patterns of social disintegration within each country were matched and paralleled throughout Europe.

What was at issue was the collapse of the hitherto accepted basis of authority and legitimacy and the failure to find any alternatives to them. The process can be seen at its strongest in Germany, where the revolution of 1918 and the abdication of the Kaiser initiated a period in which the legitimacy of the Republic of Weimar was challenged both by left and right, by Spartacists and Communists, by Kapp *putsch* and by Bierkeller revolt. The challenge diminished significantly, as did the strength of monarchism, after the election of ex-Field Marshal von Hindenberg as President in 1925,[5] though the outward appearance of stability he offered was not enough to guard against the street fighting between Nazi and Communist of 1931–2 or the rise of Hitler.

In France and in Italy there was no event as traumatic as that of the Kaiser's abdication. Neither state had established the strength of authority enjoyed by the German Kaiser. The circumstances of the birth of the Third Republic had isolated and put at enmity with it many of the social groups which would normally be expected to support an established system of government. For these the Third Republic lacked legitimacy. Its corruption, its anti-clericalism, its assault on the army at the time of Dreyfus, were irrevocably against it. After 1920 its achievements became even more insupportable. It was unable to preserve the value of money. It lost steadily to Britain in its traditional spheres of interest in the Middle East. It became dependent on Britain for peace in Europe, accepting Locarno after the failure of the occupation of the Ruhr. It accepted inferiority to Britain at sea by treaty at Washington in 1922. From the beginning of the 1930s, the dependence of France on Britain became more and more pronounced. When the efforts of Barthou and Laval to create a separate security policy based on agreements with Italy and Russia broke on the Italian–Ethiopian crisis, the Right turned more and more against the Republic.

The post-war Right in Germany, France and Italy—even in Britain—differed considerably from pre-war conservatism even of the traditionalist kind. In the first place, the demands of mass warfare had produced an officer class drawn from levels of pre-war society whose members, before 1914, could, at best, have hoped for reserve officer status, that of 'temporary acting gentlemen', no more. The Armistice and the peace settlement demobilised them, but it could not return them, least of all in their own eyes, to their pre-war status. But their new position was worthless if revolution and inflation destroyed the only society in which its enhancement was of value. To these ex-officers had to be added those age-groups which had spent their adolescence under the strain of war, seeing no hope of existence beyond their eighteenth birthday, and then being robbed of their chance of death or heroic adventure by the sudden outbreak of armistice. For these men, the war had destroyed idealism, leaving nothing unsullied to which the young might dedicate the enthusiasm and capacity for idealism which were the hallmarks of their youth. For these Garcia's words in André Malraux's *L'Espoir*, 'Transformer en conscience une expérience aussi large que possible',[6] were the best they could do; but their experiences tended to be sought in the extra-curricular activities of the *Freikorps*, the Black and Tans, or the *cadres* of European international communism.

The civil war which began in Europe as the church bells rang out the armistice was in essence a triangular conflict: traditionalist conservatives and democrats, upholding the *Rechstaat*, being challenged by those new reactionaries of the anti-parliamentary right, and by the revolutionaries of the anti-bourgeois left alike. The dimensions of the conflict can be measured by the existence of para-military organisations side by side with those of the state. They came into existence to protect those who no longer trusted or felt they could rely on the forces of the state—vigilantes, home guards, *Einwohner-wehren*, identifiable originally by neighbourhood, then by social groups and then by a generalised totalitarian nationalism. They perpetuated the phenomenon of *Grabenkameradschaft*, identification with one's unit amidst the chaos of war and revolution.[7] They perpetuated the class identification of the social *arrivistes*, 'hostilities only' commissions of the war. These were the para-military forces of demobilisation; they were to be followed by the para-military of the depression years, more organised, bound to the anti-parliamentary political parties. Of the original twenty-five members of the S A, seventeen were too young to have fought in the war. But the winning of power left them no role to play; the bureaucratised SS, rival to the German professional armed forces, fared successfully where the SA's ethos of spontaneous revolution made them an easy victim to a dictator who preferred to capture rather than overthrow the machinery of state.

The armed forces, then, faced the approach of the Second World War amidst a general and widely-spread belief that their own society in particular and that of Europe in general was dissolving into civil strife. This feeling was least developed in Britain, the occasional trumpetings of the more aged *embusquées* notwithstanding. Violence, aside from the minor brutalities of Mosley's euphemistically named stewards, was alleviated by emigration, the Palestine Police,[8] the International Brigade. By the side of the murders and shootings of the Kapp *putsch*, the General Strike was small beer and the Scapa Flow mutinies[9] symbolic rather than real. This was, perhaps, why the unfortunate Count Schwerin of the German General Staff, desperately trying to make contact with his British opposites in 1939, found himself regarded with the suspicion normally reserved for traitors from one's own side by the simple patriots of the British General Staff. Britain was caught up, willy-nilly, in the Europe-wide civil war, without much understanding, and somewhat against the general will. But in the events which led up to its transformation into international war in September 1939, the armed forces of Britain played as much of a part as those of France, Germany, Italy or Poland, and infinitely more than those of the USSR.

To sum up: it is the contention of this book that the processes which led Europe into the Second World War were both a conflict between the powers of Europe, working within a European system of states, and a conflict between separate elements in a common European society: that the role of the armed forces in the disintegration of their own national societies

is part of the role they played in the disintegration of that
Europe which their countries had in common: that that role
can be examined in the light of their ability to adapt their
methods of warfare to the technological developments through
which Europe was passing, in the light of their strategic policies
and estimates of each other and in that of their common fears
of a new European war. The examination of these separate
themes is to be the task of the chapters which follow.

2 Armed Forces Within a Disintegrating Society

During the years 1914–18 the experiences of the major European belligerents followed a very similar pattern. In each of the major powers the balance between military and civilians was severely disturbed. In Germany the army leadership, the Great Germany Military Headquarters came, under Hindenburg and Ludendorff, to exercise what was to all intents and purposes a complete military dictatorship, overriding the Kaiser entirely and thwarting and manipulating the growing power of the Reichstag and the political parties.[1] In France the habitual struggle between political leadership and the chambers had for much of the war to take second place to the struggle to assert any political authority over the military leadership.[2] In Britain the Lloyd George Coalition was barely strong enough to remove a naval leadership which seemed set on losing the war, and had therefore no moral reserves with which to take on the power and authority of Sir Douglas Haig, even after the near disaster of 1917 and the German spring offensives the following year.

Civilian authority had only been re-established among the victors at the Paris peace conference, the most strains being on the relationship between M. Clemenceau and the allied Generalissimo, Marshal Foch.[3] It is hardly surprising, therefore, that in the years which followed the peace conference, public opinion in the victorious powers swung for a time bitterly against the military establishments. Anti-militarism had been

a growing movement before 1914. After 1920 it gathered
strength and force as the military leaderships came to be in-
dicted by writer after writer, on the basis of first-hand
experiences, on charges of what amounted to mass murder by
professional stupidity. Whether the authors concentrated on the
appalling sufferings of the war in the front lines as in the work
of the British war poets, Wilfred Owen, Edward Thomas and
others, in Erich Maria Remarque's *Im Westen nichts neues*,
and in Henri Barbusse's *Under Fire*, on the barbarisation of
ordinary life and values, as in Ernest Hemingway's *A Farewell
to Arms*, Edmund Blunden's *Undertones of War*, Ernest von
Salomon's *Die Geächteten*, or on the allegedly criminal
stupidities of the High Command, as in C. S. Forester's
brilliant *tour de force*, *The General*, the picture presented to
and relished by very large sections of the intellectual, book-
reading public was one in which the losses of the war represented the last crime the military élites were to be allowed to
perpetrate upon the ordinary people of Europe.[4]

Literary anti-militarism combined with the idealisation of
the League of Nations and of Article 10 of the Covenant, with
its provisions for disarmament, to produce a decade in which
the need for armed forces *per se* was increasingly called into
question. At the political level the pressure of public opinion
for disarmament was greatly reinforced by the demand for
economy in public expenditure, a demand which, on the
political centre and left stemmed, it is true, in part from the
old nineteenth-century liberal idea that expenditure on arms was,
in itself, socially wasteful, but which sprang much more from
the desire on all sides for a return to the financial stability of
pre-war Europe.

Among both the victors and the vanquished the professional
officer corps and their leading élites were forced into the status
of a beleaguered minority, whose *raison d'être* was more and

more called into question. Visions of future wars, waged entirely with poison gas and from the air, completed the public image of them as dodos of the contemporary world, archaic survivals doomed to extinction; perhaps not dodos, however, since they were still far from harmless in the eyes of the left in Britain and France, where militarism came to be associated more and more with the rising tide of Fascism.

These processes put a severe strain on the loyalties of the military élites. The process of negotiating for disarmament, it has been said, is the transfer of warfare to the negotiating table. Its rationale, that international security can be maintained at the same level of confidence at all levels of armament provided the ratios between one nation's armed forces and those of her political adversaries remain the same, fails to carry overwhelming logical conviction even to the layman. Few military advisers accepted it for a moment, since for them there was always a minimum level of security irrespective of the relative strengths of their political enemies. The coupling of the pressure for cuts in existing levels of armaments with an international security system which included, under Article 16 of the Covenant, an open-ended commitment to employ national security forces anywhere, at the bequest of the League Council, made complete nonsense in military terms, as the British Chiefs of Staff pointed out in a famous memorandum of 1923.[5] Paradoxically, the pressures towards 'perpetual peace through perpetual war' exacerbated both civil–military relations within the states who participated and relations between these states, too. It was an American press correspondent, reporting on the Geneva Naval Conference of 1927, who had to be reminded by his editor that he was not reporting a war.[6] The rebuke could well have been directed at any of his European colleagues.

The armed forces of Europe thus found themselves more and more alienated from the states and societies in which they existed and which they served. These societies were at the same time undergoing severe internal strains as their economies sought adjustments to the disruptions and weaknesses set up by the war and its aftermath. To the more simple-minded military the Italian catch phrase, *'il mondo va a sinistra'*,[1] raising the spectre of socialism and Bolshevism, summed up a world in which order, authority, legitimacy and patriotism seemed increasingly to be losing their public appeal and acceptability—it was not foreign enemies but internal subversion, ideas rather than bullets, that seemed to threaten their world. Many of them failed to recognise that the real threat came, not from the radical anti-nationalists of the left, but from the nationalist radicals of the right, the attractiveness of whose sentiments hid a series of aims which were to prove much more destructive of the values and loyalties of the professional soldier than the anti-militarism of the left.

In their intellectual isolation amidst the uncertainties of the 1920s, the professional soldiers of Europe tended to react according to one of three patterns: that of the professional soldier, that of the political soldier or that of the super-patriot. The professional sought moral self-approval in abstention from politics, becoming a *'Nur-soldat'* in the German phrase, a 'fighting soldier' in the British. The professional soldier, while at best grudgingly admitting the necessity for this second category, regarded the willingness of the political soldier to co-operate with, to 'play the game' of an essentially non-military, if not anti-military, civilian establishment, as despicable and in the long run self-defeating. To the super-patriots, whose politics were declaratory, not manipulatory, alliance with the anti-political movements of the right, especially those with leader figures which might in some way supply the personal focus for loyalty, lost with the disappearance of absolute monarchy in Europe, was the only way to protect the nation and the army.

Such soldiers tended to embarrass the professional and the political soldiers alike, and to be early candidates for superannuation or economy cuts. Their immediate reappearance in the ranks of the anti-political movements went a long way to confirm liberal and left-wing opinion in its inability to distinguish between military men and militarists, or between either and Fascists.

The experience of the French armed forces between the wars epitomises these processes. The role of the army in French politics had always been difficult. It was, as its defenders never ceased to remind the French public, the oldest French institution, much older than the Third Republic, with traditions rooted equally in the armies of the monarchy, the Revolution and the Empire. In essence, it betrayed its divided origin, being an uneasy alliance between the republican idea of the citizen army, the nation in arms,[8] and the tradition of a professional army with an officer class drawn from the hereditary landowners, the catholic nobility. As such it had been through one hundred years or more, since the whiff of grape-shot of Vendémiaire and the expulsion of the deputies on 18th Brumaire, the bulwark of the party of order against the party of movement. It had cleared the streets of Paris in June 1848, suppressed the commune in 1871, and broken in turn the wine-growers in 1907, the Paris general strike of 1908 and the miners of the Nord in 1911–13. Since 1848 it had been regarded as the class weapon of wealth and the social order. Suspicion of the standing army and its replacement by a true citizen militia, a temporary *levée en masse*, had been an essential element in every progressive programme from Gambetta's electoral campaign of 1869 to Jean Jaurès' *Armée nouvelle* of 1910. True to the revolutionary tradition of the career open to the talents, there had always been much promotion from the ranks. But promotion beyond the rank of major had been largely confined to the graduates of St Cyr or the *Ecole Poly-technique*, preserves of the nobility and the *grande bourgeoisie*.

The French army had seen its holy status as the guardian of the national honour and hope of *revanche* broken over the Dreyfus case and its senior officers purged in favour of those whose Freemasonry guaranteed their loyalty to the Republic. Its cherished doctrine, the superiority of the moral over the material and of the attack over the defence, had been obliterated by 1916, together with the flower of its pre-war officer corps. The military mutinies of 1917 had produced a Pétain quiet and long-suffering, in the place of the devotees of Foch and Grandmaison. Foch's return to favour as the Allied Generalissimo had produced military victory at the cost of new and heavy losses, but it was a victory whose effect had been whittled away both at Versailles, and by the failure of the army-sponsored Rhenish separatist movement and Poincaré's invasion of the Ruhr. The financial disasters which followed hit the officer class of the post-war army particularly badly. In 1919–20, much of the surviving elements of *nobilité* and *grande bourgeoisie* among the officer corps had removed themselves by large-scale resignations.[9] The post-war officer class tended to come from the middle and small bourgeoisie and from the prosperous farming classes, with fixed salaries and capital held in government bonds. The inflation which defeated Poincaré and brought about the success and subsequent disintegration of the *Cartel des Gauches* hit those groups particularly badly. The increases in taxation felt necessary to counter the inflation and the consequent inquisition into personal finances of the bureaucracy reinforced the hostility of the officer corps to the parliament, to the Republic and to the former Anglo-American allies 'massed against our finances'.[10] Returns to agriculture fell badly, ground rents in 1934 being worth barely half of their value in 1914.[11] Officers' wives were forced to take jobs. By the mid-1920s the crisis of morale in the officer corps, with all chances of promotion blocked by the top-heaviness of the senior ranks stuffed with wartime appointees, and faced with too many tours of colonial duty in Morocco, Syria or Indo-China, had reached crisis point. In 1926, Painlevé wrote, 'The Army is at present the prey of a deep uneasiness. Its *cadres* are dispirited and look for an opportunity to leave the service. The young turn away from our military schools.'[12]

The atmosphere was made worse by the machinations of the French parliamentary leaders. Military service had been reduced to eighteen months in 1923 and in 1928 was cut to one year. The erection of the Maginot Line became a military necessity when the annual intake was only just over 100,000 men, due to fall in the 1930s to 70–80,000, and the fulltime professional army was reduced to not much more than training *cadres* for the annual class and the most available reserves. To man the Maginot Line fully required the full conscript class, a ready reserve of 143,000 and 50,000 regulars out of the total regular strength of 136,000. This was a measure short of full mobilisation, it is true, but under its title, the *couverture*, clearly more than an ordinary peacetime force while at the same time (as General Weygand, Chief of the Army Staff wrote in 1932) standing at 'the lowest level consistent with the security of France in the present state of Europe'.[13] There was, in Léon Blum's words, an annual ritual, by which the military budget was cut all along the line before reaching Senate and Chamber for further cuts. It could hardly fail to convince the new Chief of Staff that the basic desire of the parliamentarians was to republicanise the army and leave France defenceless before a renascent Germany. Indeed, his own appointment in 1930 had given rise to parliamentary criticism so hostile as to force him to appear before his critics to defend himself.[14]

The French picture of German rearmament was, as we shall see in a later chapter, grossly exaggerated. The German army had come more recently than the French—to be accurate, on 9 November 1918—to the state of dissociation with the German state that had haunted the French army since 1870. Being, however, unencumbered by any revolutionary traditions it had found a solution much more quickly, although this was to prove no more permanent than that of France. During the war the *Grosse Hauptquartier* of the army and the duo, Hindenburg and Ludendorff, had come to exercise a very real dictatorship in Germany,[15] against which neither the Kaiser nor the Reichstag could prevail but with whom both were forced to co-operate. As formal head of state and focus of the personal oaths of loyalty of the officer corps, the Kaiser was as essential to Germany as the Mikado to Japan. The Kaiser's sudden abdication on 9 November 1918 deprived Germany of legitimate government and the officer corps of any focal point for loyalty.[16] At the first meeting of Ebert's Cabinet on 10 November 1918, when Erzberger asked for plenipotentiary power to sign the armistice at Compiègne, the Ebert Government lacked any authority to grant him such powers; it lacked, too, any wherewithal to maintain itself in power.[17] The action of General Groener, who had the previous day not only told the Kaiser flatly that the army would obey its generals and commanders but that it did not acknowledge the Kaiser's orders any more but had also blocked a proposal that the Kaiser should abdicate only as Kaiser and not as King of Prussia,[18] is well known. Critics of the Social Democratic leadership by the score have attacked Ebert for accepting Groener's offer of army support as making a genuine democratic Germany impossible. One may be forgiven for doubting whether the disintegration of all Germany into the kind of civil war conditions that obtained in Bavaria and of the German army into *Freikorps* of left and right would have served any genuine democratic purpose. What is important for our study, however, is Groener's motive for turning to Ebert, the need to give the officer corps a new focus for its loyalties and to conjoin these loyalties 'not to a particular form of state but to Germany'[19] to which he added in 1925 'the restoration of a government based on law, armed support against its enemies and the opportunity of calling together a National Assembly', impeccably democratic sentiments surely.[20]

The German officer corps of which General Groener was to take such care had suffered losses as severe as any. In 1914 there had been 23,000 regular officers and 29,000 reservists. By 1918 there were 46,000 regulars and 226,000 reservists. 11,000 regulars and 35,000 reservists were killed so that by 1918, eleven-twelfths of the officer corps were either not regulars but 'hostilities only' or were newly commissioned.[21] Under such conditions the group ideals of the regular officers could have been totally swamped. What saved the German army was the terms of Versailles and the imposition of the 100,000-men army. The organisers of the new army were able to take their pick of the survivors of the 1914 regular officers, especially into the embryo General Staff. The remainder of the officer corps they drew from senior and medium-ranking regimental officers, younger regulars with General Staff appointments, wartime regular officers with battlefield command and the group known as Noske-lieutenants, about 1,000 long-service NCOs given commissions by the law of 9 March 1919. The effects of this policy were that by 1934 the only major changes in the social composition of the officer corps was that the proportion of sons of landowners had fallen from just under 10 per cent in 1913 to just under 5 per cent in 1934, that of sons of businessmen and industrialists from 15 per cent to 9.5 per cent and those of sons of regular and reserve officials and of former NCOs had risen from 24 per cent to 34 per cent and 4 per cent to 8 per cent respectively.[22]

The officer corps preserved its internal cohesion partly because of the rigid imposition upon its members of the concept of *Überparteilichkeit*, total abstention from politics, a measure which Groener, both in 1918 and during his period as War Minister after 1928, saw as essential to the avoidance of any kind of left–right polarisation of opinions among the corps; and partly because the old Prussian military tradition had emphasised loyalty to Church as much as to Kaiser. With the disappearance of the crown, the churches became of increasing importance. Up to 1936 only Catholics or Lutherans were accepted into the officer corps and the chaplains were an indispensable part of the bonds which kept the individual units together.

The Weimar Republic led a short and troubled life. It failed to command the support of important sections of German society at all levels from the *national-gesinnte* judges who made holes in its laws to protect the violent men of the right[23] to the sizeable German communist movement with its consistent use of street violence and its occasional attempts at armed revolution. As the German historian, Golo Mann, has written 'that which could never integrate itself, with the best will in the world could not integrate the army'.[24] The army remained encapsulated in itself, an estate in the medieval sense, separate from the rest of the nation, with its own standards of 'authority', its own sense of institutions and its own feeling of honour.

Two sources of strain on the armies of the victors were kept from the German army by a third action. The *Diktat* of Versailles meant that there was never any serious conflict between army and civil authority over disarmament and little, if any, over any but the smallest details of foreign policy, although the army abrogated to itself executive authority in this field in relations first with Soviet Russia and later in 1933–36 with China.[25] The second was the absence of any real conflict between *Nursoldatentum* and nationalist sentiment. This latter conflict was to come; but only as a consequence of the rise of Nazism, and of the very belated realisation by sections of the officer corps and the General Staff that a nationalist movement, professing the same goals as did the army leaders themselves of rebuilding the nation and the army—might intend to command the army, use it and indeed integrate it into the movement in a way which would threaten the existence of the army as such, whether the aim were crowned with victory or came to defeat.

Überparteilichkeit was, of course, never prescribed for the army leadership. General von Seeckt, it is true, held the army apart both from the Kapp *putsch* and from its suppression. Thereafter he kept the state at a distance until his own conception of his powers brought him into conflict with it. But his successors, Generals von Heye and von Hammerstein, sought to reduce the distrust and General Groener, as *Reichswehrminister*, felt himself forced to bring the army leadership into politics to protect the army from the anti-militarist left. But it was from the anti-parliamentary right that the real threat came in the subversion of loyalties of the junior officials revealed in the Scheringer trials in 1930. And the collapse of the parliamentary republic in 1930 made the intervention of the political officer, General von Schleicher, and his final betrayal by the blackmailing of von Hindenburg and the pliability of General von Blomberg, inevitable.

The German armed forces found themselves faced in 1930 with the dilemma to which the Italians had already succumbed: disintegrating public order, a collapse of ordinary political government and the threat of an imminent *coup d'état* from a party not only sympathetically disposed towards the army's own grievances but one which had absorbed many of their former comrades.[26] Italian failure to contain Fascism stemmed, however, from the much weaker position occupied by the army in Italy, a country which had never succeeded in attaining the social cohesion to correspond with its political unification. The Italian officer corps remained sundered from the social élite of Italy (its members themselves regionally divided) by its Piedmontese origins and its commitment to an anti-clerical state. Service in the army conferred status and the *bella figura* so essential to Italian self-esteem on an officer corps, sharing in the shallowness of aims of the Italian bourgeoisie from which the political leadership itself rose. And the collapse of Italian political leadership amidst the disappointments and defeats of the peace settlement was paralleled by a similar collapse in the prestige and appearance of the officer corps. Large-scale demobilisation threw on the economy not only the 'temporary gentlemen' with wartime commissions who graduated naturally into the ranks of the para-military organisations of the right, but also substantial numbers of the generals, left destitute on no pay or at best inadequate pensions. While d'Annunzio was holding the headlines with his Fiume adventure, the Minister of War was recalling Italian troops from Albania and Anatolia on the grounds that the internal conditions in Italy did not allow the maintenance of troops abroad, and General Adolfo Tettioni, Chief of Supplies for the whole Italian army from 1915 to 1918, died of starvation in Turin, demobilised on a pension of fifty lire a day.[27]

In these moments the Italian military leadership was obsessed with status and appearances. The Commander-in-Chief, General Diaz, attended the Prime Minister, Nitti, not to advise him on the best way to deal with d'Annunzio's insubordination but to solicit a nation's gift of two million lire and the title of Duke of Vittoria.[28] And the future Marshal Badoglio, whose career in the war had not led to the command of an army, least of all the victorious command of an army, lent his services to Nitti's disgusted attack on the army in return for promotion to Chief of Staff and the appointment of Diaz to an honorific powerlessness.[29] Ten Ministers of War in three years revealed the contempt Italian politicians had for the armed forces and for military policy. During that period Badoglio continued his intrigues. And Mussolini's Fascist forces used the plight of the army as a stick with which to beat the succession of parliamentary governments. The officer corps clung to its only lifeline, its loyalty to the crown rather than the state. The Fascist organisation seemed patriotic and invulnerable; and Mussolini was careful not to call the position of the crown into question. The army leadership was equally careful to assure Victor Emmanuel that they would defend Rome despite the army's unalterable sympathy for Fascism: verbally General Diaz told the king the army would do its duty, but it would be better if this were not put to the test.[30] The march on Rome was not opposed. Indeed, several generals, including de Bono, took part in it. Mussolini rewarded Diaz by putting the army completely into his hands, and Badoglio, who for once had backed the losing side, sought refuge for a time as ambassador in Brazil.

The German General Staff was made of much sterner stuff. In 1920, it is true, von Seeckt had held the army aloof from the Kapp *putsch* with the remark, 'the Reichswehr do not fire on the Reichswehr'. But when in 1923 the officer cadets and men of the Infantry School at Munich supported Hitler's attempted Bierkeller *putsch*, it was treated as mutiny excusable only in the peculiar circumstances of Bavaria in 1923, as an example of what could happen if the young soldier was exposed to too much politics.[31] Von Seeckt demanded total abstention from politics. And when von Hindenburg's election as President in 1925 set at the head of the new state a man who had already, during the was years, served as a kind of Kaiser substitute, von Seeckt's own intrusions into politics cost him his position.

What disarmed the General Staff in 1932–3 was the collapse of the Weimar parliamentary regime under the attacks of the Right, in full cry against the Young Plan and enlisting in their support the anti-parliamentary forces of Nazism and the SA. The young officers, schooled to regard being non-political as synonymous with nationalist, *national-gesinnt*, listened more and more sympathetically to Nazi attacks on the Weimar system. Few went as far as those sentenced at the trials of 1930 for spreading Nazi propaganda, but their sentencing aroused widespread sympathy for them. Von Hindenburg spoke slightingly of Hitler as the Czech corporal, *der bömische Gefreiter*. Groener saw the issue simply as one of discipline. In 1932, when he held the position both of *Reichswehrminister* and Minister of the Interior in the Brüning Cabinet, he carried through the suppression of the SA. The new military leadership of von Schleicher and von Hammerstein was not prepared to support him against the political storm his action aroused in the form of the misgivings of the divisional commanders. Von Schleicher's own ambitions led him to conceive the idea of making the Nazis, now the second largest party, the political instrument of an army dictatorship. He was, however, unable to induce Hitler to fall into the obvious trap, despite his re-legalisation of the SA. Nazi–Communist co-operation in the Berlin strikes of October 1932 raised the spectre of disorders too great for the army to contain. The Chancellorship was eventually forced on von Schleicher; and instead of his dividing the Nazi party, the *camarilla* around von Hindenburg were able to blackmail the old man into accepting Hitler as Chancellor.

Hitler himself, meanwhile, had found, through the agency of Colonel von Reichenau, Chief of Staff to the East Division, a senior military figure—General von Blomberg—who was willing to play his game. The senior officers of the army, apart from von Schleicher's direct supporters and a small group whose religious connections had already turned them against Hitler, were as much affected by Hitler's apparent determination to restore direction and authority to the government of Germany as were the junior officers. The disintegration of German political life, the second through which they had lived in fifteen years, clearly demanded a new order, a new system. It seemed for the time being that this had been found in Hitler. The position of von Hindenburg, the appointment of von Blomberg as *Reichswehrminister*, and Hitler's authorisation of a rapid build-up in the armed forces all confirmed this. Enlightenment was to be a long time coming.[32]

By contrast with the trials and tribulations of the German, French and Italian armed forces, those of Britain had a remarkably easy time, although this is hardly how they would have described their experience at the time. The British officer corps was unique among those of Europe at the time in that its social role was not challenged, its conception of order hardly disturbed, and its integration deep into the machinery of government unique. Socially the army leadership was conservative and concerned with the maintenance of British power. But this was far more likely to be challenged in India than in Britain; and the principal victims of the absolute use of military power were the Irish and the Indians. The reluctance of the army leadership to subject their troops to the strains of maintaining order against a hostile citizenry was an important factor in the defeat of the policy of repression by the Sinn Fein and the IRA in 1920–22. And the fate of General Dwyer, author of the Amritsar massacre, was a warning against the hazards of military action against civilians even in India. Troops helped or stood by during the General Strike: but they were unaffected in loyalty even by the spectre of a Labour government or the pressure on the navy to accept a level of forces which effectively ended the period of British naval supremacy. The one issue that had shaken the loyalty of the officer corps before 1914—Ulster —from which so high a proportion of the military leadership was drawn, remained untouched. Before 1922 the Coalition Government of Lloyd George was effortlessly outmanoeuvred by the political leadership in Ulster. After 1922 the domination of the Unionist party in Ulster was too important an element in the electoral strategy of the Conservative party for it to be raised again.

The real strength of the leadership of the armed forces in Britain lay in its recruitment from broadly the same milieux from which the civilian élites drew their members, with perhaps a larger bias towards the landed gentry than was true of the élites as a whole: and in the complete integration of the highest levels of the military leadership with their civilian counterparts through the machinery of the Committee of Imperial Defence.[33] Its Secretary, Colonel Sir Maurice Hankey, was also Secretary to both Cabinet and Privy Council.[34] And the invention of the Chiefs of Staff Sub-committee, carried through by the first Labour government under the advice of Hankey and with the curious reappearance of Lord Haldane as, in effect, Labour's Minister of Defence, crowned this integration. Civil–military relations in Britain were thus able to survive the strains of demobilisation and post-war economies, of disarmament to a level which left Britain virtually defence-less against her potential enemies, of the Geddes Axe, the Ten Years Rule, and the cuts in pay which accompanied the financial crisis of 1931. The Scapa Flow mutinies of 1931, significantly confined to the lower decks, were a consequence

of incompetent management and were not repeated elsewhere.

The problems Britain's armed forces faced were concerned,
not with their existence, but their effectiveness; save only
for the mythological, if not pathological battle provoked in
1920–22 by the conviction of the founders of the new independent Royal Air Force that the two older services were
dominated by the sole idea of dismantling the Air Force into
its original components, the Royal Flying Corps and the Royal
Naval Air Service, and subordinating the air to the demands of
older, more conventional forms of warfare. Trenchard, the
first Chief of Air Staff, made himself the spokesman of the
somewhat futuristic notions of those who believed that air
bombing had put an end to conventional land and air warfare.
In fact the strategic deterrence he preached was beyond the
primitive technology of air warfare in his time. And his insistence on doctrinal rigidity cost the Navy any chance of
participating in the development of air warfare at sea, impeded
the development of Singapore, prevented any chance of the
Chiefs of Staff developing a common strategic doctrine or viewpoint and awoke civilian fears of attack from the air which
were to make a considerable contribution to the hesitancy with
which Nazi Germany and Italy were treated in the early 1930s.

The advent of Hitler to power, the Japanese defiance of the
League over Manchuria, the break-up of the World Disarmament Conference and the abortive Nazi putsch of July 1934 in
Vienna in which the Austrian Chancellor, Engelbert Dolfuss,
was murdered, marked a major change in the security system
in Europe. Up to that point, the armed forces in Europe had
worried about their task of maintaining the security and defence
of their respective countries in an abstract sense only. From
1933 onwards, the spectre of war in Europe, this year, next

year, in five years or in ten, haunted their sleep and dominated their waking hours.

Hitler's coming to power in Germany was at first largely welcomed by the officer corps. The new *Reichswehrminister* insisted on a strict interpretation of the *Überparteilichkeit* originally proclaimed by Groener and von Seekt, an interpretation which forbade any interference with the Nazi revolution, whether it was directed against the residual powers of the states, or against the political parties, trades unions or other political institutions and organisations. *Gewehr zu Fuss!*—'Stand Easy' —was the army's standing instruction, even including a prohibition on aiding those who sought sanctuary with the army.[35] Protests from those whose religious or constitutional convictions enabled them to recognise that this political neutrality was making possible the establishment of a tyranny of which the army would soon be the victim, were subjected to the severest of pressure to keep silent.[36] The leading officers *were* able to secure that von Schleicher's supporters were replaced, not by von Reichenau and similar pro-Nazis, but by professional soldiers such as Generals von Fritsch and Beck. And the following year they saw, as a reward for their adoption of an antisemitic purge of their number and the addition of the swastika to their insignia, the suppression of the SA.

This suppression was accompanied by a number of political murders, including those of Generals von Schleicher and von Bredow. These events were followed almost immediately by Hindenburg's death and the fateful ceremonial oath of personal loyalty to Hitler himself taken by the entire Army singly and severally.[37]

The bulk of the officer corps and the army leadership seems to have been simply overtaken by these events without realising their full significance or having the opportunity to concert any objections against Hitler's extraordinary unconstitutional action. Resistance began to gather against Hitler first of all in the field of foreign and military policy. Until the programme of accelerated rearmament, undertaken on Hitler's instructions in February 1933, began to pay off, it was, in the view of the army leadership, essential that German foreign policy should be calm, unprovocative and at all costs directed towards the avoidance of conflict. Moreover, every measure must be taken to prevent Germany becoming isolated diplomatically and being made the target of military pressure.[38] Hitler's policy of week-end *coups*, even where this resulted in the adoption of conscription and the remilitarisation of the Rhineland, struck the army leadership as irresponsible and unwelcome. The orders of 2 May 1935 for a staff study on the military preparations necessary for a sudden pre-emptive strike against an unnamed south-eastern state (obviously Czechoslovakia)[39] led General Beck, the Chief of the Army Staff, to threaten his resignation with the sentiment that 'a military leadership' which undertook such an adventure 'would deserve the harshest condemnation not only from its contemporaries but from history also'.[40]

With this, the second round of Army opposition to Hitler— the first since his achievement of power—had begun. Characteristically, it expressed itself in an internal struggle between the Army Command and the new Supreme Command in process of creation by officers sympathetic towards Nazism. The need for such a Command which would unite the three armed services was obvious. Equally obvious from a strictly constitutional point of view was the need for political control over the armed forces as well. But Goering's *Luftwaffe* with its own ministry and a minister who was heir to the Nazi succession was uncontrollable. And the German navy flatly refused to have anything to do with a unified command. The battle that developed was confined therefore to the army, to a conflict between the traditionalist view that the Commander-in-Chief of the army and the Chief of Staff were the responsible military advisers of the state, and that their responsibility extended to the political aspects of the policies on which they were asked to advise, and the view that their role was purely technical and executive, and that in a state run on the *Führersprinzip*, command by the political leader, there was no place for any doctrine of military co-responsibility.[41] This was the view taken first by General von Blomberg as Minister and, on his fall and the replacement of the Ministry by the OKW, by Generals Keitel and Jodl, its professional heads. The row began in 1934,[42] continued bitterly over the issue in June 1937 of the 'Orders for the unified preparation of the armed forces for war'[43] and took on new force when the report of Hitler's address of 5 November 1937 to the military commanders in chief, the Hossbach Protocol,[44] reached Beck's ears. By then he had already flatly refused to take any action on that section of the June Orders that envisaged a *coup de main* against Austria in the event of a Hapsburg restoration—special case Otto.[45] The scene was set for the long conflict of 1938, with which we shall deal in a later chapter.

The main characteristics of the army's conflict with the Nazi leadership in the 1930s was that it developed essentially over questions of German foreign policy and estimates of the reactions to that policy of the other European powers. That the policy at issue was revisionist, violent and essentially anarchical in a European context was equally the issue in Italy, France and Britain, though in each case it was conditioned by the particular experience of the military leadership in each country during the 1920s.

In Italy, for example, Mussolini had achieved power, not so much in alliance with the army, but by buying the abstention of the army by a promise to respect its position. His first

ministry included the victorious comrades of the war, Armando
Diaz, and the naval commander, Thaon di Revel. Since Mussolini's view of the state was essentially manipulatory, the army
was thereafter left undisturbed. The leadership settled down to
confirm the privileges and interests of the officer class, leaving
both policies and military development (which would have
needed an active military policy and risked civilian control) to
one side.[46] Mussolini's repeated rhodomontades on the glory
and power of Italy's armed forces hid the fact that the main
capital expenditure was going into the navy and the air force.
The Chiefs of Staff of the three services became dependent on
Mussolini, who occupied the three Ministries of War, the Navy
and the Air Force from 1925 to 1929 and again from 1933 to
1943. And Badoglio, who had recovered Mussolini's confidence
sufficiently to become Chief of the General Staff of the armed
forces in 1925, was content to retain control over the army and
leave the other two services to themselves. In 1927 he added
the Governorship of Libya to his prizes, multiplying his
honours while reducing his influence to nil. Mussolini organised the Ethiopian enterprise through the Ministry of
Colonies and with the co-operation of the Chief of Staff of the
army, over Badoglio's head.[47] Otherwise he gave no long-term
strategic directives to the Chiefs of Staff, nor did they demand
them, contenting themselves with their own theoretical exercises and hypotheses.[48] This continued right up until the
Italian entry into the war. And deprived of strategic directives
the generals could only express their anxieties in the void, or to
their would-be allies. The German audience for Marshal
Pariani during his visit to the country in the summer of 1938,[49]
the German military attaché in Rome,[50] the German partici-
pants in the staff talks of April and June 1939,[51] heard far
more of these anxieties than Mussolini ever did.

In France, the appointment of General Weygand as Chief

of Staff to the army in 1930 marked the intensification of the civil–military struggle to its bitterest and most severe.[52] In these years the internal strains on the Third Republic were greatly increased by the belated spread of the worldwide depression to France, by the actual summoning of the Disarmament Conference, by the need to accept an end to the payment of reparations by Germany as well as by the rise of Hitler to power in Germany and the immediate intensification of German rearmament. The Versailles system seemed doomed. Weygand saw himself as the defender of the army and the nation against those who worked to destroy them. As Foch's right-hand man and spiritual heir he had never accepted the legalism of Versailles as a proper substitute for that superiority of French forces which alone, in his view, could prevent the revision of the Versailles territorial settlement and the destruction of peace in Europe. He set his face, therefore, against any measure of disarmament whatever. The argument that France could not afford to be isolated diplomatically, let alone shoulder the responsibility for the failure of the Disarmament Conference left him, though not Gamelin, who was to be his successor, unmoved. The politicians' idea that a true collective security system (with inspections), breaches of which would leave France free to act (an idea Gamelin supported),[53] he saw simply as a plot to weaken France's effectiveness, already, in his view, at the lowest margin compatible with French security.

The conflict that developed had as its background a continuing decline in the authority of the parliamentary and governmental system of the Third Republic which was proving incapable of containing Germany, of maintaining the economy, even of maintaining internal order. In 1932, the index of national production fell 20 per cent, national income shrank, the deficit in the balance of payments rose threefold, there were suddenly a quarter of a million registered unemployed.

In 1934 the Daladier Government cravenly resigned in the face of the Paris street riots, although it still commanded a parliamentary majority. In 1935 the foreign policy of the Government of 'National Concentration' swallowed German denunciation of Versailles before breaking entirely over Ethiopia. There followed eighteen months of chaos in industry as the Popular Front was confronted with working-class demands for the 40-hour week. The result was that the army saw—and failed to recognise—an immense accretion of power to itself through the simple weakening of the civil power. In practice this meant that as the army was still without the power to initiate a new defence and rearmament policy, for which parliament remained the only responsible body, because of the weakness of parliament and government no new policy was initiated. For lack of any possibility of providing an alternative, the conservative arms policy of the past was continued. Weygand might have defeated the politicians; but the bureaucracy which duly cut the military budget was a different matter.

Weygand's conquest of the politicians can best be illustrated in the debate over France's effective strength. By the late 1930s it was expected that the annual intake of conscripts would fall to between seventy and eighty thousand, reflecting the low birthrates of the war years. It was generally agreed that an extension of service to two years was politically impossible. The alternative was to stagger the current call-up, which would weaken the current number of effectives but add to those in the future. The *Loi Bernier* of 1933 was introduced to give effect to this. Already France's forces had been dangerously weakened. The reserve divisions were skeletons of what they should be. In December 1933 Weygand arraigned the Premier, Daladier, before the Conseil Supérieure de la Guerre.[54] Confronted with the authority of France's three marshals Daladier withdrew, humiliated. In outrage Parliament passed the *Loi*

Bernier. But the Daladier Government fell within the month. The Doumergue Cabinet which succeeded it included Marshal Pétain as War Minister. The *Loi Bernier* was repealed. But Pétain did not feel strong enough to insist on two years' service. When Weygand retired, his successor, Gamelin, had to negotiate with Parliament the right in times of national emergency to retain the annual classes with the colours beyond their normal period of service. And Daladier, who soon returned to the Cabinet and to the Ministry of War, rarely sought to activate the machinery for civil–military consultation thereafter. The military remained beyond civilian control. When, in January 1936, M. Flandin demanded of the army the preparation of plans for an armed riposte in the event of a German military incursion into the demilitarised Rhineland, Gamelin simply procrastinated until Hitler turned Flandin's fears into reality.[55]

France thus entered the vital years of 1938–9 with a military that had acquired a virtually independent position within the state by virtue of the increasing weakness of the civilian power, but that had accepted as the price of that acquisition the inability to react positively to the threat from Hitler either by a new alliance policy or a new policy of rearmament. The army's nemesis came in 1940 when it proved capable of surviving the military débâcle, but at the cost of being involved, not in a genuine national renewal, but to that obscene parody of French nationalist dreams, the Vichy state. Small wonder that many of the younger officers turned to the para-military leagues, the *Croix de Feu* or the *Union Nationale des Combattants* or that when the Cagoulard conspiracy was broken up, it was found to have ramifications within the army as far upwards as Colonel Groussard of the personal staff of Marshal Franchet d'Esperey, or General Duseigneur. The members of the Army Council found themselves on that occasion forced to pledge their individual honour to Daladier, once more Minister of War, that they had no connections with the conspiracy.

The French army preferred to take refuge from the rising threat from Germany in a state of self-encapsulation which made them guardians of the nation *in* defeat rather than *against* it. Although machinery existed for civil–military consultation[56] it was sparingly used and never achieved the integration of civil and military planning that existed in Britain. In this Britain was extremely fortunate. Civil–military divisions did exist, it was true. They arose at a time when the Chiefs-of-Staff machinery was failing to function. Not that its members were at daggers drawn, as in the days of Admiral Beatty, Lord Milne and Lord Trenchard: Admiral Lord Chatfield's chairmanship of the Chiefs of Staff was marked by that command of management and compromise that had distinguished his entire career. But the consequence of the Beatty–Milne–Trenchard era was that the three services had developed three quite separate strategies for three quite different wars, only one of which—the Admiralty's fears of Japan—had much political validity, but all of which, however, had at least served the purpose of arguing the annual battle of the estimates with the Treasury.

The armed services had borne the brunt of the Treasury cuts manfully throughout the lean years of the late 1920s and the starvation of 1931–2. But when the Chancellor indicated that he expected enough of a surplus to permit some repair of the deficiencies incurred in the past, and the Defence Requirements Sub-Committee of the three Chiefs of Staff, together with Sir Maurice Hankey in the chair, Sir Warren Fisher for the Treasury and Sir Robert Vansittart for the Foreign Office, was set up to advise the Cabinet on how this surplus should be spent, the Chiefs of Staff failed abysmally The political section of the report was clear and remarkably accurate in its prognostications.[57] The Chiefs of Staff produced three separate shopping lists, predicated on their three alternative strategies, which together totalled a third as much again as the anticipated surplus. Fisher, whose contempt for the Chief of Air Staff was even more monumental than that which he felt towards the CIGS, intervened with the Cabinet to impose a common strategy. The army was denied a Continental expeditionary force, the navy its dual standard against Japan and Germany, and the air force found itself saddled with an air defence of Great Britain which ran flatly contrary to its belief in the strategic bombing offensive. Fisher, Air-Marshal Dowding and Sir Robert Watson-Watt's radar saved Britain in 1940. But the common strategy imposed by Treasury fiat and maintained throughout the 1930s was a civilian strategy which answered neither the needs of British diplomacy nor the demands of the services. The conflict was eventually however one about priorities. As such its story belongs to a later chapter in this book.[58]

At the opposite extreme to Britain, with its unified élite, lay the Soviet Union. The Red Army in 1933 was a powerful and progressive army, making impressive innovations in its use of airborne troops and its development of mass armoured tactics. Its new officer corps was an amalgam of the radical and professional survivors of the Czarist armies and the new entrants produced by the civil wars and the emergence of a Soviet educated élite. In 1934, though still firmly under party control, it had won comparative immunity from the system of political commissars imposed on it in the early days. It had survived two purges unscathed. It was acquiring a professional cohesion —inspired, no doubt, by the example of the Reichswehr with whose forces it was in clandestine contact, though these contacts were broken from the Russian side in 1933.[59] There are still vast areas of ignorance in our knowledge of this, the first

Soviet peacetime army; but it is clear that in the Soviet state it was the only form of élitist social organisation that could in any sense stand comparison with the position of the party.[60]

It now seems reasonably well established that there were some clandestine contacts between officers of the German General Staff and their Red Army equivalents in 1935-6. The evidence suggests that the Reichswehr representatives, unofficially exploring the possibilities of a renewal of the Rapallo policy of the 1920s, were greeted with reserve by their Russian contacts[61] at precisely the same moment as Stalin was approaching Hitler for a *détente* through the intermediary David Kandelaki, the Georgian head of the Russian trade mission in Germany.[62] Whether Stalin got word of these German contacts and decided to rid himself of those who were anticipating his own turn of mind or whether an elaborately faked dossier was planted on him by the SS we shall possibly never know.[63] But the effect was to launch him on the military side of the great purges and to destroy the existing High Command, over half of the trained staff corps and the chain of command down to brigadier level, and to decimate the entire officer corps.[64] With this he destroyed any credibility the Soviet Union might have enjoyed as a worthwhile ally. The shambles of the 1937 manoeuvres[65] and the Russian setbacks at Japanese hands in 1937 and 1938 in the Far East underlined this.

There remained the question how far the disintegration of society in Germany, France and Italy, and the apparent disintegration of Europe as a whole, led to any comparable change in the attitudes of the military élites to Europe considered as a society. Military men are, by tradition and training, xenophobic, patriots rather than internationalists. Against this one can place the feelings of the more politically minded for their allies in past wars or for their potential allies in the future. Such feelings, as experienced by the advocates of a Russian connection in the Reichswehr, or by the pro-French and pro-American groups in the Royal Navy tend to be bilateral, devoted to a single other nation rather than to some larger concept. More important in this context was the general prevalence of a loose anti-Bolshevism in all the European armies. This led some into sympathy with Fascism (the more eccentric even into the advocacy of a native Fascism) and others into seeing Russia as the main enemy. The desirability of a Nazi–Soviet conflict is a not uncommon theme in military small-talk in Britain and France in this period.[66] Few, however, went so far as the egregious Group Commander Winterbotham,[67] the air force expert in the Secret Service, with his assiduous cultivation of Alfred Rosenberg. More significant, perhaps, is the emergence among the German military opposition to Hitler, first of an appeal to the traditional political morality of Europe against the crass and nationally selfish use of military power envisaged in Hitler's foreign policy, and then to the first hesitant and tentative contacts with representatives of Britain and France. These contacts vary from the attempt to induce Britain to follow a policy most likely to reinforce German internal opposition to Hitler to the provision of military intelligence on a scale indistinguishable from old-style treason. This was justified as the salvation of the real interests of the German nation from those of the regime which was betraying them. (The same justification was made for Weygand's defeatism in 1940.) This, however, is a theme to be developed in a later chapter.

3 New Doctrines and Technologies: Military Conservatism and Technological Change

In the first chapter I made the point that the status of the individual states in the European political society depended to an important degree on their ability to defend themselves against foreign attack. This ability is a function of three factors: the geographical vulnerability of the frontiers of each state, the strength of its industrial and economic base, and the size and efficiency of its armed forces. In nineteenth-century Europe, the relative combinations of these factors as perceived by the other states in the European system had produced what was called a balance of power, a device which, up to its breakdown in the first decade of the twentieth century, had preserved general security, though it had been unable to prevent various bilateral conflicts for nearly a hundred years. It is important to note in this context that, even in 1914, the objective factors on which the balance was based had not failed. The contestants were far too closely matched for anything but a monstrously destructive stalemate to result from the war. What had changed were people's perceptions of the balance.

In those one hundred odd years, the military forces of Europe had met and mastered a considerable degree of technological change. The railway, the rifled gun, the machine-gun, barbed wire, the steamship, armour plating, refrigeration, canned food, high explosives, electricity, the field telephone, the motor car, long-distance cables and wireless, had, one by one, swum into the ken of the military, gradually informed their approach to war, met with resistance from military conservatives and finally became part of the accepted machinery of war. There is some evidence to suggest that from the 1870s onwards the rate of technological change had accelerated beyond the capacity of the military to adapt. Certainly one of the most apparent sources of the appalling casualties suffered by all sides on the Western Front was the failure of the General Staffs to appreciate the effect on the standard field tactics laid down in their military manuals of the heavy artillery barrage, barbed wire and the machine-gun. The Russo–Japanese war had afforded clear evidence of all three of these new phenomena. But the lessons had simply not been studied or, where studied, they had not been absorbed. The First World War was to produce four new technological developments: the military aeroplane armed with bomb and machine-gun, the cross-country armoured vehicle with tracks rather than wheels, the lorry and poison gas. The last proved a chimera. It was too easy to counter, gave no side an advantage, was prepared but, by tacit consent, never used in the Second World War. The other three developments were used, if at all—the Germans never took to tanks—for most of the time as adjuncts to conventional warfare. Only if the war had lasted another year would the world have seen an effective and original use of the new weapons on a scale adequate to reveal their full capabilities.

The Second World War in turn produced four major technological developments, each startling enough to make for overwhelming victory. The first was the combination of armour and dive-bombing aircraft which made the German army victorious in Poland, France, Jugoslavia, Greece and, until November 1942, in Russia. We call it the *Blitzkrieg*. The second was the combination of radar with the fast, single-wing, all-metal heavily armed fighter aircraft and the ground-to-air telephone which won the Battle of Britain in 1940 and with-stood the deep penetration of the RAF and the USAAF over Germany in 1943. The third was the large aircraft carrier with dive-bombers and torpedo-bombers which wrecked the American Pacific fleet at Pearl Harbor, swept the Royal Navy from East Indian waters, and nearly from the Indian Ocean too, and then was met and defeated by its own kind at the battles of the Coral Sea and Midway. The fourth was the atomic bomb.

There were other minor developments: the jet fighter; the long-range flying bomb and missile; the submarine-heavyship combination used so devastatingly by the Germans against the ill-fated PQ 17; the magnetic mine; Dönitz's wolf-pack sub-marine tactics; the schnorkel submarine and so on. But they either came too late in the day or they were met and defeated by the scientists who served each side. They are significant merely in that they demonstrate convincingly the importance which technological development and its masters, the 'boffins', had acquired for each side. The battle winners, nearly the war winners, were those developments which caught the other side unprepared and unable to adapt quickly to the new way of warfare. This lack of preparation or of adaptability stemmed in the first three cases from the tenure of an alternative doc-trine, a doctrine whose strength depended on the role the armed forces had come to occupy in their own society.

THE BLITZKRIEG

Let us begin with the *Blitzkrieg*. Its essential elements were the cruiser tank, fast and armoured to withstand light artillery fire, and the flying artillery, the dive-bomber, trained to close co-operation with the armour and available to be called upon to blast any body of troops in field fortifications that stood in the way of the armour. To the tanks were added motorised assault troops, infantry and engineers, riding into battle on armoured carriers, if not on the tanks themselves. A later refinement, especially where command of the skies was not assured, was the self-propelled assault gun. A still later refinement, used with devastating effect in Normandy, was the rocket-firing ground attack aircraft. These were, however, all refinements on the basic combination.

The term *Blitzkrieg* hardly appears in the professional literature before the German conquest of Poland in 1939. And indeed the employment of aircraft in combination with tanks was only finally accepted in Germany in the winter of 1938-9. But the idea – sudden, overwhelming attack with the aim of victory as soon as possible—is central to German military thinking since the genesis of the Schlieffen Plan.[1] Only by the speedy defeat of the enemies on one frontier could the spectre of German defeat through a two-front war be exorcised. German military commentators on the events of August–September 1914 agreed generally that what had gone wrong with the Schlieffen Plan was its execution, not its conception. As the military forces of the defeated nation, determined on recovery of its losses, the German armed forces were therefore open, almost from the moment of defeat, to any military development which promised a return to the war of movement and an end to trench warfare, especially the avoidance of a multi-fronted war. There were considerable doubts as to whether this would prove possible. But with its desirability no one was found to quarrel.

The idea of making warfare mobile again was one common to all the armed forces of those who signed the Armistice of 1918. This was the dominant philosophy of the British tank corps, preached to it incessantly by its first Chief of Staff, Major-General Fuller, and incorporated by him into the strategic planning for the 1919 campaign during his service at GHQ, France. Personal difficulties, and his conviction that the tank had superseded or should supersede all other arms of the army, made his career less important than that of Captain Sir Basil Liddell Hart, who came to the tank after the war, from an elaboration of the role of the infantry in the attack, which had already developed two of the fundamental principles of the *Blitzkrieg*: high concentration on the point of attack and the pouring of an 'expanding torrent' of forces through the point of breakthrough in a rapid and deep strategic penetration.[2] On the French side, General Jean Estienne had come to advocate a separate tank force in studies made for the French army in 1919–21 and had drawn up specifications for the French heavy B1 tank.[3] In Germany Colonel Guderian had pounced almost at once on Liddell Hart's paper 'A New Model Army' that appeared in the *Army Quarterly* in 1924, two years after its rejection by the CIGS, the Earl of Cavan, as too contentious; Guderian had had it translated at once into German.[4] Cavan's successor, Lord Milne, was more open-minded. Having read Liddell Hart's *Paris or the future of war*,[5] he authorised the creation of an experimental armoured force. Sheer lack of money and the competing claims of other branches of the army limited the effectiveness of much of the experiments carried out, although they did lead to the first official manual issued by any army on armoured war. Both this manual, the *Purple Primer* as it was commonly known, and its successor, the 1931 *Modern Formations*, divided the army into mobile divisions and infantry divisions, with light and medium tank brigades mingling with horsed troops in the mobile brigades.[6] And after the 1934 manoeuvres, widely believed to have been 'cooked' by the cavalry men, the army embarked on the mechanisation of the cavalry rather than the expansion of the Tank Corps. Only in 1937 were the cavalry definitely transformed into light tank regiments and it was even proposed to take the medium tank out of the mobile division entirely. The effect, however, was to check any development of tank types and the issue of new specifications.[7] The British tanks throughout the Second World War were thus to be one generation behind their German (and Russian) equivalents in gun calibre and range.

The British experiments had however been followed with interest by opinion on the Continent. Colonel Guderian had been lecturing on mobility since 1924 and General von Seeckt had become sufficiently interested to press for the establishment of a tank centre as part of the facilities granted to the Reichswehr by the Russians.[8] Dummy tanks were used in the 1927 manoeuvres. Five German prototypes, all slow, lightly armoured and equipped only with 37 and 75 mm guns (First World War infantry tanks, in fact) were tested in Russia in 1929.[9] At that time the Soviet tanks were very similar. General von Blomberg, then head of the *Truppenamt*, had criticised them for being too slow during the 1928 exercises at Kiev.[10] The Soviet army shared the German preoccupation with mobility and the offensive, Voroshilov's 1929 Field Service Regulations talking in terms of large numbers of tanks being used for a breakthrough.[11] But the idea of independent tank divisions being used for deep strategic penetration came to both Germans and Russians in the years 1931–2 under the impact of Fuller's Haldane Lectures of that year,[12] Liddell Hart's studies of Sherman's campaigns in the American Civil War[13] and the arrival in Russia of sixty British tanks, including the Vickers Medium. This was capable of 15–20 miles per hour across country, and so for the first time gave reality to the theoretical speculation of the tank addicts.[14]

In 1931, General von Lutz became Inspector of Motorised Units and took on Guderian as his Chief of Staff. It was under their direction that specifications were issued for what became Panzers III and IV, the principal types used by the German army up to 1943.[15] In 1934 Lutz and Guderian published the first comprehensive, German-language work on armoured warfare, the Austrian General Ludwig Ritter von Einsensberger's *Der Kampfwagenkrieg*, a full-blooded advocacy on Fullerian lines of the tank corps and tank army. In 1935 the General Staff exercise of May at Bad Elster studied the use of a whole Panzer corps; the following year, the use of a panzer army was studied.[16]

At that date the British first tank brigade under General Hobart was conducting experiments in deep strategic penetration. Guderian was able to work the results of these experiments into manoeuvres in July 1935 at Münster. Three months later the first three Panzer divisions were formed. That, however, was as far as Guderian could take the new arm for several years. The 1936 manoeuvres on the Vogelsberg were an infantry exercise, involving five divisions and only one battalion of tanks, used in an infantry-supporting role.[17] The 1937 manoeuvres in Mecklenburg involved nine infantry divisions and one Panzer.[18] So, it was only in April and May 1938, after the *Anschluss*, that two further Panzer divisions were added, with three light motorised on the British model the following November. That month, however, Guderian was made Commander of Mobile Troops, a new position created by Hitler, with direct access to the Führer. By reducing the number of tanks to a division from 433 to 299, he managed to create the nine Panzer divisions that defeated France with a total of 2,574 tanks and armoured cars.[19]

In these years the Soviet tank corps was the only one to keep pace with the Germans, if indeed it was not somewhat ahead.

In 1932 the Soviet BT high-speed tank units were being developed for long-range penetration. And Soviet ideas of industrialisation were being reproduced in military writings on the 'war of the machines' and the development within the Soviet mass revolutionary wing of the élite motor-mechanised armies. In 1932 the Soviet Union had over two thousand tanks.[20] And the 1936 Field Service Regulations contained a section on the use of tanks in mass attack and for deep penetration and encirclement of enemy forces which looks, at first sight, pure Fuller.[21]

This is, however, illusory. The Soviet High Command was as divided as that of the other European countries. The Soviet tank corps existed in a framework of manned infantry and artillery and a fascination with *matériel*. Tukhachevsky himself, shortly before his fall,[22] published a long and hostile critique of the Fullerian mistakes of Soviet tank advocates, in not realising that tanks could not operate successfully without mass artillery support. And in 1939 the seven mechanised corps were dissolved, as a result of what is now widely recognised in the Soviet Union as a misreading of the lessons of the Spanish Civil War.[23]

The Soviet authorities were not the only ones to draw a mistaken conclusion from the Spanish Civil War. The defeat of Franco's forces at Guadalajara, where he used large numbers of armoured vehicles, was hailed by French writers as showing the superiority of the anti-tank gun over the tank,[24] a doctrine which was to do nothing to accelerate the development of tanks in France or the transition from the DLM, the light motorised division, to the tank division. As a result, although France in fact had a slight numerical superiority in tanks in 1940 over Germany and a very considerable advantage in tank types, this was of no avail.[25]

The armoured offensive and the deep penetration practised

by the German armour after the breakthrough at Sedan in May 1940 is only one part of the success of the *Blitzkrieg*. The other is the substitution of the dive-bomber for the heavy assault gun which, at least before General von Leeb's insistence on its development paid off in Russia in 1941–2, was un-motorised and comparatively immobile. Here again the Royal Air Force and its predecessor, the Royal Flying Corps, had held the lead, the employment of ground attack with light bombs and machine-guns having been one of the most effective British restraints on the German infantry offensives of spring 1918. These techniques had equally been used by the RAF in its imperial policing days in Iraq, on the North-West Frontier in 1918–19 and in the Aden Protectorates. They had, however, no place whatever in the doctrines of the Royal Air Force, obsessed as its High Command was from 1922 onwards with strategic bombing and the strategic deterrent.

The German *Luftwaffe*, independent, Nazi, the direct expression of the second most powerful man in Germany, Hermann Goering, is at first sight the last place one would expect to find the development of a doctrine of battlefield co-operation with the army. Here, above all, one would anticipate that denigration of the traditional arms and that embroidery of futuristic scenarios which distinguished both the Italian theorist Douhet and Lord Trenchard. The *Luftwaffe* did in fact go through a Douhetian phase in the years 1933–5 under the influence of the first commander of the *Luftkriegsakademie* and of its first Chief of Staff, General Wever.[26] However, Wever's death in 1936 removed the main advocate of pure air warfare just as the *Luftwaffe* was having its nose firmly rubbed in the limitations imposed on such theorising by the current state of air technology, by the difficulty of hitting any target on the ground accurately and by the immediate needs of German defence against enemies on her frontiers, France,

Czechoslovakia and Poland; to bomb these countries, long-range strategic aircraft were simply unnecessary. Spanish Civil War experience seemed to suggest that civilian morale was a lot firmer under bombardment from the air than Douhet or Trenchard would ever admit. The inadequacies of existing bombing sights led to concentration on dive-bombing with pin-point accuracy. Shortage of petrol and oil resources in Germany argued again for the same step-by-step conquest that Hitler was already planning, in which each defeated country provided one with bases for attacking the next. The demands of air warfare theorists were thus met, without destroying the basis of the army–air co-operation on which army advocates of the *Blitz-krieg* laid so much stress. Destruction of the enemy air force in the opening days of the fighting, attacks on military concentration areas, stores, etc., were all that was called for. Destruction of the sources of wealth and industry in the enemy country would also remove much of the loot potential—and economic rewards for aggression played a large part in Hitler's motivation. Against Poland, the *Luftwaffe* was forbidden to attack the centres of economic activity unless an immediate military necessity existed. The *Luftwaffe* was thus prepared for a short war, its front-line strength being backed by very little rearmament in depth. And its failure can be seen in 1940 against Britain, when its inability to win command of the air from the Royal Air Force meant that the invasion was never launched.

Against the ground attacks of the *Luftwaffe* on land, however, neither Britain nor France succeeded in developing any counter. The loss of command of the air over the battlefield in 1940 and 1941, which, whether in Norway, France, Greece or Crete was basically a fault of bad organisation or preparation, left the troops on the ground comparatively unprotected against the combination of tanks and aircraft. The Stuka dive-bomber could, however, only operate when the air battle had already been won. Thereafter it was equally effective against warships as against land targets, as the Royal Navy learnt to its cost off Greece and Crete. The Royal Air Force never developed its own dive-bomber. The ground attack techniques of 1944, though practised by the RAF as much as by the USAAF, were of American development.

Britain and France were prevented from either appreciating the danger of the techniques under development in Germany or developing their own brands of mobile warfare by their conviction of the superiority of the defence. In the case of Britain this conviction came fairly late—at the military level, that is. Ever since the investigations of 1919–20 into the lessons of the First World War, French military doctrine had been dominated by two ideas. The first was the superiority of the defence in advance of, or at the very least on the frontiers of, France. The offensive could only succeed if it could muster a superiority of at least three to one manpower, six to one in guns and fifteen to one in ammunition fired. The First World War had been won by fire-power and by Allied superiority in *matériel de guerre*: as Weygand wrote in 1938 'the tyranny of material imposed by the omnipotent power of fire'.[27] Since France's areas of greatest industrial wealth and activity were within easy reach of the German frontier, this made the holding of the frontiers without retreat of redoubled importance.

From these ideas emerged the doctrine of the continuous front, extending the full length of France's frontiers. Fixed permanent fortifications, moreover, would make up for France's inferiority in manpower to Germany. The answer, therefore, was the Maginot Line, a belt of fortifications running from the Rhine to the Ardennes where the Belgian fortifications would continue.[28] Just as the machine-gun had doomed the frontal infantry attack to costly failure, so the anti-tank gun would doom frontal attack by tanks to a similar fate. If Germany were not actually deterred from attack on France and Belgium by the prospect of attacking such fortifications, she would face inevitable heavy losses and, once the blood-letting had weakened her sufficiently, the victorious counter-offensive.

These doctrines, as has been argued in an earlier chapter, gained an added strength as a result of the internal political position secured by the army after 1934. At this point the parliamentary vigour necessary to the major rearmament pro-gramme which the evolution of a more offensive strategy would have required was simply lacking. After 1936 and the defection of Belgium into neutralism, French misgivings as to their ability to withstand a German *attaque brusquée* grew. But the weakness of the French armaments industry[29] and the improb-ability of a major change in French military policy, which would involve a confession of error so great as to deliver the army into the hands of its radical critics, led to an almost hysterically exaggerated repetition of the old doctrine. Of this General Narcisse Charvinceau's *Une invasion est-il encore possible?* (a question answered only a few months before the German breakthrough at Sedan with a resounding negative) is the best known example.[30]

British belief in the superiority of the defence was, unlike that of France, of 1930s vintage, and lacked any basis in the experience of the First World War or the manoeuvres of the 1920s. Captain Liddell Hart himself carries a good share of the responsibility. His studies of motorisation had brought him by 1935 to the belief that it would favour the defence by adding mobility to the machine-gun and the anti-tank gun. In works such as *When Britain Goes to War* (1935), *Europe in Arms* (1937) and the *Defence of Britain* (1939) he expressed such views as: 'it is a common assumption that attack has usually paid in the past. This is contrary to the balance of evidence. Analysis shows that in the majority of battles which are engraved on the pages of history the loser was the army which was the first to commit itself to the attack'.[31]

It may be added that because the British army was committed to the proposition that the defeat of France would be a strategic disaster for Britain and that in any campaign in France, the French military contribution would be so very much larger than the British one that France would dictate the course of battle, there was little it could do but adopt the French strategy: just as to support France meant, inevitably, conscription and a large expeditionary force.

There is a temptation to ascribe the triumph of military conservatism in France and Britain over those who advocated the development of ways of warfare based on the new technology to the narrow social basis of the French and British officer corps, and the determination of its members to keep out anything which might threaten its social cohesiveness. This kind of populist approach, very prominent in the writings of the people's army advocates of 1940–41 in Britain,[32] is very largely nonsense and ignores the fact that both the military radicals of the inter-war years and those who successfully adapted the experience of 1940–41 to victory in 1943–5 came from the same social milieux as those they supplanted. If the French army rejected de Gaulle's call for an all-mechanised élite Army of the Future, advanced in his book of the same name in 1934,[33] it was precisely its élitist, long-service professional character, a flat contradiction of the whole French myth of the nation-in-arms, which most ensured its rejection. Similarly, Liddell Hart's call for a six-division, all-mechanised army, the 'Gold Medal Army' of the 1936 RUSI prize essay of that name, made political nonsense in a situation where what was needed was less arms than an assurance to a France feeling itself increasingly weak and beleaguered that it was no longer alone. In purely military terms, the introduction of conscription in May 1939 no doubt, made very little sense. In political terms its effect would have been much greater a year earlier. But essential it undoubtedly was.

AIR DEFENCE

The danger of seeking an easy sociological explanation becomes the more striking when the second of the major technological victory-winning developments here chosen is examined. This is the combination of radar, single wing, high-speed fighter and ground-to-air radio telephone which won the Battle of Britain. It was an entirely British development, achieved in the teeth of the dominant British air force doctrine. That doctrine, built up by Air Marshal Lord Trenchard, Chief of Air Staff from 1918–28, insisted that the aircraft was a weapon of offence not defence, and that unless the utmost strength was employed to insist on that doctrine, civilian fears of air attack might well prevent the best use of air power. On the basis of the effects of the German bombing attacks on London in 1917, Trenchard maintained that in air attack the moral effect was much greater than the material in a proportion of about twenty to one. Fighter defence, in his view, should be kept to the lowest possible figure as a concession to the weakness of civilians. The way to victory was to defeat the enemy nation rather than its armed forces. This uncivilised and defeatist nonsense, which led directly to Air Marshal Harris's wholesale destruction of German cities, stemmed from a conviction of the general beastliness of war and the consequent desirability of as strong a deterrent and as speedy a solution as possible, once the deterrent had failed.

It was a doctrine that had little room for the air defence of Great Britain and held little hope, once enemy bombing forces had been allowed to achieve numerical superiority in the air over Britain. Hence, until 1938 the successive Air Ministry plans for rearmament in the air sought mathematical parity with German air strength even to the point of building at considerable expense many hundreds of aircraft which were obsolete even before their completion. Not until 1938 when parity *per se* seemed clearly out of Britain's reach was the Air Ministry forced as a whole to think about defence. By then Fighter Command was two years old and the Spitfire and the Hurricane were under development. The Air Ministry was not, however, prepared to order them off the drawing boards.

The Ministry had been forced to accept the development of fighter defences and of Fighter Command by the Treasury as the price of Treasury consent to their own bomber plans. This pressure began with Sir Warren Fisher's role on the Defence Requirements Sub-Committee and the Cabinet reception of its report. It continued through the second and third DRC reports in 1935, the Treasury Minute of 1936 and the establishment of Sir Thomas Inskip as Minister for the Co-ordination of Defence in 1936. Fisher himself acted largely as Inskip's Permanent Under-Secretary and the call in December 1936 for an ideal scheme of defence, the rejection of the first draft of the Air Ministry's scheme J in the spring of 1937 and the later insistence on priority for fighters in Scheme M adopted in November 1938 were either Fisher's entirely or owed a great deal to his inspiration. His surviving papers carry one constant theme: Britain is vulnerable, as never before in her history. This threat comes from the air. Until Britain has built up her air defences, there can be no strength to Britain's foreign policy.[34]

Fisher's insistence would, however, have been pointless without the invention of radar. The orthodox insistence that the bomber would always get through was based on a very simple equation. By the time enemy bombers, flying at 15,000 feet and over, could be seen off Britain's coasts, their speed would carry them over London before the existing fighter types could climb to the requisite height to intercept them. Experiments with audio-location were extremely unhelpful except at equally close ranges. Radar by contrast offered the identification of hostile aircraft as such at ranges of up to forty miles. Its development took place in conditions of maximum secrecy, and even when the radar towers, 250 feet tall, were erected around Britain's south-east coast, their true import was not understood by the Germans. It needed the capture in France of an installation provided by Britain as part of the Anglo-French alliance and not destroyed by the French to put the Germans on the right lines.

The development of Britain's air defence system is an outstanding example of the importance of timing. In 1940 the production of Hurricanes and Spitfires was adequate to cope with the battlefield rate of loss, there were enough trained crews to withstand the casualty rate and the radar chain was complete and had had a year's operation to attain maximum efficiency. Since the *Luftwaffe* did not understand its purpose, it had not developed any scientific counter measures. Two years earlier, one squadron of Hurricanes and one Spitfire were operational but only up to 15,000 feet as the oxygen masks had turned out to be defective. The radar chain was hardly begun. The elaborate network of command centres, plotting the movements of forces on both sides was only in process of creation.[35]

The French position was still worse. In 1938 the French air force possessed not a single modern fighter capable of matching the speed of the German bombers. The great air force of the 1920s was totally obsolete. The early 1930s, the period of gestation in Britain, had been a period of total inactivity on the part of the French army of the air, an inactivity still far from properly explained. Blame has been attached to the nationalisation of the French aircraft industry in 1936 by the Popular Front regime of Pierre Cot, but this neither prevented the industry from evolving excellent prototypes in 1937–8, nor should it have affected the proper ordering of new aircraft types in 1933–4, the period in which the RAF were persuaded to adopt the Spitfire and the Hurricane. An examination of the French experience leaves one with the conviction that it was that of Britain which was unique. The French failure was compounded by military incompetence and bad organisation. This more than anything else is responsible for the extraordinary paradox of the pressures brought on the British Cabinet to commit the reserves of Fighter Command to the Battle of France at a time when anything up to 1,500 French fighter planes were lying around central France unused.[36]

The events of 1941–2 were to reveal that the *Luftwaffe* was as ill-prepared for air defence as any air force, despite the technical excellence of its ME 109s and 110s. The explanation lay in precisely that same concentration on army co-operation and the short war that made its units such effective partners to the German armour in the *Blitzkrieg*. Goering's ill-timed boast that no enemy aircraft would get through to Berlin was the product of ignorance—an ignorance itself produced by the absence during the 1930s of any enemy within striking distance of Germany with an air force and a strategic doctrine of any danger to Germany.

This is perhaps worth underlining in view of the exaggerations still put about by critics of the British abandonment of Czechoslovakia in 1938. While the prospect of major air attacks on German cities by Soviet aircraft based on Czechoslovakia would almost certainly have had a deterrent effect on Hitler's plans for Czechoslovakia in 1938, not only is there no trace of any apprehension of such a development in the German military planning, but the Soviet air force set no store by theories of strategic bombing. As the opening phases of the 1941 campaign in Russia were to show, it was as overladen with obsolete aircraft as ever the French or Italian air forces were. It did, however, have the capacity, the design skill and the allies to repair this deficiency. Like its fellow services, the Soviet air force was disastrously affected by the purges. Khripin and Alknis, who had developed Soviet bomber forces and played about with Douhetian ideas only to refute them in the name of the 'unity of all fighting arms', the dominant Soviet military cant, were purged and Tupolev the designer, imprisoned.[37] Poor Soviet bomber performance in the Spanish Civil War, the fault of local conditions and commanders, may have been held against them. Their successors were Loktinov, a non-entity, and Smushkevich, a brilliant fighter pilot, with no experience of commanding anything larger than a wing. Their appointment coincided with the drying up of American help, reabsorbed into the American aircraft industry with the latter's recovery from the 1937 depression. Soviet aviation entered an era of prototypes—the disaster of 1941 was an adequate reflection of this.

More extraordinary than the failures of the other major air powers to evolve efficient air defence programmes is the Royal Air Force's official and alternative doctrine of defence through counter-bombing or the threat of it. The counter strike force had been official doctrine in the RAF since its formation. Before 1937, however, it had been a matter of oriental reiteration, a kind of strategic Om-Mani-Padmi-Hum, never related to any specific opponent save for the brief period in 1922 when the French air peril loomed over London. In the spring of 1937, the future Air Marshals Harris and Slessor, led an examination of the application of air force doctrine to Germany.

They discovered that they had no idea of what was operationally possible, what targets could be reached or how they could be hit, what effect the existing bombs would produce, what effect would be produced on the targets or what the casualties from enemy fighter forces would be. The capacity to hit and destroy German industry simply did not exist.[38] A year later, on 19 September 1938, Air Chief Marshal Sir Edgar Ludlow-Hewitt, Commander of Bomber Command, suggested that the Command could do nothing without bases in France and admitted that only fighters and AA guns could defend London.[39] For nearly twenty years the Air Force High Command had been preaching a strategy without reference to its operational possibilities, a strategy of the Emperor's clothes being preferred to one of cutting one's coat to fit the available cloth.

NAVAL WARFARE

The last example of technological victory-winning developments lies in the Japanese and American development of long-range naval warfare based on carrier-borne dive-bombers and torpedo-bombers. The only European powers to be met with this were Britain and the Netherlands, as the French possessions in South-East Asia were occupied by Japan without naval engagement. But before those disasters the Royal Navy had learnt its own hard lessons at the hands of the *Luftwaffe*'s dive-bombers, and made one strikingly effective use of seaborne aircraft against the Italian navy at Taranto.

The failure of the Royal Navy to develop practices analogous to those of America and Japan was in part a product of geography, in part an offshoot of the same preoccupation of the Air Force High Command with theories of strategic deterrence.

Geographically the vast spread of British naval stations through-out the world meant that the Navy was never properly seized, as were the Japanese and Americans with their Pacific preoccupations, with the problems of long-distance warfare. In 1924, Admiral Sir Herbert Richmond wrote from his temporary command of the East Indies station to Lord Haldane:[40] 'Ask them', he wrote (referring to the newly developed strategy of naval concentration on Singapore in the event of trouble with Japan) 'what they intend to do with the battle fleet once they get to Singapore.' The suggestion was that current naval thinking simply cut off at that point. Certainly, the Air Staff had never devoted a moment's serious thought to the demands of war in the Far East, save for Lord Trenchard's attempts to pre-empt the defence of Hong Kong and Singapore for the Royal Air Force.

The significance of this lay in the control exercised between 1918 and 1936 over naval air forces by the Royal Air Force. The naval component of the RAF during this period attracted no attention from the Air Staff, once the battle for its control had been won from the Salisbury Committee of 1923. The pilots and observers were in fact trained naval officers who stayed with the service when it was returned to the Navy in 1937.[41] Even then it was only the actual seaborne aircraft that returned to the navy. All land-based aircraft co-operating with the navy remained in the so-called Coastal Command of the Royal Air Force. The failure to develop any real theories of the use of air power at sea is directly traceable to the largely fallacious bomber versus battleship controversy of the early 1920s, revived in 1936 as part of the Air Ministry's last ditch defence against the naval building programmes of battleships and aircraft carriers of 1937-8. Apart from that failure, this period of control and neglect was equally reflected in the technological backwardness of British naval aircraft, the Swordfish biplane and the Skua fighter/dive-bomber being hardly the equivalent of the land-based aircraft which they might expect to meet in combat. The valiant and, with the loss of HMS *Glorious*, tragic story of the Fleet Air Arm's operations off Norway is adequate illustration of this.[42]

Naval doctrine in fact regarded the role of the Fleet Air Arm as one of reconnaissance to be used, in addition, on occasion for action against enemy warships so as to bring them to battle. Taranto and the actions against the *Dunquerque* in Oran were regarded as exceptional, the 'proper function of the Fleet Air Arm', in the rather defensive words of Captain Boyd of HMS *Illustrious* after Taranto, being 'the operation of aircraft against an enemy in the open sea'.[43] This is perhaps best illustrated in the air attacks on the Italian battleship *Vittorio Veneto* which, in each case, were flown by single flights of half a dozen aircraft or so from HMS *Formidable* whose full complement of aircraft was seventy-two. The idea of a Japanese or American carrier using its forces in such penny packets is unthinkable. Indeed, only necessity of the direst sort would have sent a Japanese or American carrier as the single component of a major surface striking force. The hunt for the *Bismarck* was to reveal a similar paucity of material, HMS *Victorious* being able to fly only six Swordfish and two sub-flights of Fulmars and HMS *Ark Royal* only fifteen Swordfish at each strike, the others having to be used as long-range reconnaissance aircraft. It took the disaster of the *Scharnhorst* and *Gneisenau's* break through the Channel, unstopped by the sacrifice of six Swordfish, all that the Admiralty could spare to stop an enterprise which they had anticipated, to call public attention to the supply of aircraft to the Fleet Air Arm. From 1942 onwards the Fleet Air Arm was entirely re-equipped, almost completely with American machines. In the landings in North Africa, Sicily and Italy and southern France, and in the final stages of the war in the Pacific, in operations against Palembang, Okinawa and the main Japanese islands, the Navy showed its thorough digestion of the American experience, using its carriers in a group, flying air attacks of fifty to eighty aircraft at a time. A far cry from the single carrier sent to Singapore in winter 1941, which was saved from the débâcle which overtook the *Prince of Wales* and the *Repulse* by its accidental running aground in Durban harbour.

So far three examples of technological developments have been considered, the failure to adapt to which brought defeat on land to France, in the air to Germany and at sea to Britain. The first cost France her freedom and destroyed the Third Republic. The second ended the westward drive of the Third Reich and drove Hitler eastwards against Russia and into eventual defeat by superior forces. The third cost Britain her Asiatic empire. The question in each case must be whether this failure to adapt was coincidental or whether, as the theme of this book suggests, it stemmed from structural defects inherent in the internal divisions of national society.

In the French case, the failure to adapt to the possibilities of the *Blitzkrieg*, a failure which was even more palpable in the air than on the ground, seems to have been inextricably involved with the French army's view of itself as the alternative embodiment of the French nation and people. Its apotheosis amidst the parades of Vichy makes it impossible to call it a democratic view. It was, however, certainly a view of the nation as a whole, élitist only in its belief in the mission of the army to lead. Such an army could not accept the total separation from the people which would have been involved in the abandonment of conscription and the adoption of a professional long-service army on the Seecktian model as advocated by General Charles de Gaulle. Nor was it ever happy as the servant of the regime. Hence its inflexibility of thought and doctrine became institutionalised and beyond the power of the weakening governments of the 1930s to impose upon.

By contrast the British failure to adapt to the tank, after leading the world in its invention and development requires a more complicated explanation. In part, it was a question of finance, in part a reaction to the wholist claims of the extreme tank advocates, in part a reflection of the élite position of the cavalry officers in army society, a position which led to general motorisation as the salvation of the cavalry regiments rather than to the expansion of the Royal Tank Corps. More important, however, was the general determination of civilian strategists not to allow the generals to design a continental expeditionary force, a determination which largely ruled out tank expansion since tanks were thought rather ill-designed for the colonial wars which were all the army were allowed to plan for before the winter of 1938.[43]

Both France and Britain accepted that the anti-tank gun was to the tank as the machine-gun to the infantry, ignoring the lack of development or supply of effective anti-tank guns to their forces. Neither country developed anything to match the German 88 mm gun originally designed to be used against aircraft.

German successful adaptation to the *Blitzkrieg* and German failure to anticipate the British air defence techniques stem from the same source, the obsession with an offensive and a short war which originated before 1914 in fears of a two-front war and was reinforced by the Nazi leadership's inability to manage the German economy without copious and regular injections of foreign loot. In this doctrine, practice, political revisionism and Hitler's own instincts for leadership reinforced each other at all levels.

Britain's successful development of the air defensive was

made possible by the freedom of traffic of ideas and personnel, institutionalised in the whole structure of the CID and Cabinet Office network of committees, between the military, the civil servants, politicians and scientists. Without radar, the Spitfire and the Hurricane, it would have been nothing. All three were ideas originally developed outside the official world, though with what were for those days considerable injections of official money. The willingness of the scientific world to co-operate in official policy is a reflection of the adaptability of the ruling élites to these new entrants, a reflection of the openness of a society which has always been prepared to recognise talent as one of the ways into its ranks.

THE ATOMIC BOMB

It is when one turns to the last of my four examples, that of the development of the atomic bomb, that the universality of European society is once more displayed. The nuclear physicists responsible for the discovery of the structure of the atom moved, in the years before the war, like iron filings in a changing magnetic field, from one centre to another: now clustering around Rutherford's laboratory in Cambridge, now at Göttingen, Munich or Berlin, now scattering to laboratories in their own countries. They came from Russia, Japan and America as well as from Britain, France, Switzerland, Germany, Italy, Denmark, Hungary, Poland and Austria. In the 1920s such movement was free. But from 1933 onwards Europe's disintegration struck there also. Max Born and James Franck left Göttingen in 1933 as a result of the SA's anti-semitism. Peter Kapitza was lured back to Russia and kept a prisoner in a beautiful laboratory, equipped very largely by the generosity of Lord Rutherford from what he had used at the Cavendish. Leo

Szilard and Edward Teller left Germany, sensitive as Hungarians must be to the smell of tyranny. Enrico Fermi left Rome in 1938 to accept his Nobel Prize in Stockholm and did not return. Others took refuge in the Soviet Union to perish in the purge or, if saved by Western protest, as were Houterman and Weissberg, to be preserved for delivery to the Gestapo in 1940.[44]

It was among these refugee scientists that the first anxieties began to arise when the experiments of Mme Joliot-Curie in Paris had been finally accepted and verified by Otto Hahn, showing uranium and radium to be fissionable. It was in fact one of them, Lisa Meitner, Hahn's former collaborator, in exile in Stockholm with her nephew, O. R. Frisch, who published the vital article in *Nature* in February 1939.[45] If a chain reaction were possible, releasing enormous amounts of energy, a weapon was also possible which would give Hitler a chance at the world domination he craved. Some American physicists, at Szilard's urging, began to operate a self-imposed censorship against citizens of totalitarian states. The censorship could not be maintained: but at the same time scientists in Britain, Germany and the United States began to urge the dangers and the need for research on their governments. At that time, as the German physicist, Heisenberg, later remarked, 'twelve people might still have been able, by coming to mutual agreement, to prevent the construction of atomic weapons'.[46] After 1945, Carl von Weizäcker remarked: 'The fact that we physicists formed one family was not enough. Perhaps we ought to have been an International Order with disciplinary powers over its members.'[47]

The critical developments came from the French team, two of whose members, Halban and Kowarski, were evacuated to Britain with their vital supplies of heavy water in 1940; and from the British, greatly reinforced by the refugees, Frisch,

Rudolf Peierls, Josef Rotblat, and Max Born's favourite pupil, Klaus Fuchs.[48] Their work was delivered to the United States in 1942, where it came under the increasing control of the nationalistically minded General Groves. In 1945 America was able to pass laws denying any of the results of the subsequent developments to Britain, in flat breach of Churchill's agreement with Roosevelt.[49] Nuclear fission had gone nationalist and lost the remainder of its European origins. Even the European refugees seemed to have taken on, in many cases, the paranoia of nationalism—as witness Edward Teller's harrowing of Robert Oppenheimer.

But it was too late. The freemasonry of science had been preserved in the muddled minds of a handful of European scientists who had joined the Communist party at the height of its anti-Fascist activities. Alec Nunn-May, recruited at Cambridge in the early 1930s, Klaus Fuchs in the late 1930s, Bruno Pontecorvo, the Italian, are those whom we know to have passed some of the 'secrets' of their work to Soviet agents. European society at its most misguided had had its revenge on the new super powers and the secrecy their armed forces sought to impose on science.

4 The Strategic Policies and Postures of the Powers, 1933-1939

The nineteenth-century European states system rested on the military balance between the major powers. Eventually it was a stable system, though it was not always perceived as such. The General Staffs of the powers kept an over-apprehensive eye upon their neighbours. That eye might vary from the gentleman in knickerbockers peering through field glasses from behind a bush in the classic table game, *l'Attaque*, to the more fantastic activities of a Mata Hari. But it made it fairly difficult for any of the major powers to steal a march on their rivals. Apprehension, despite Erskine Childers and William Le Queux, came from news of increased military budgets or naval construction programmes. It came, too, from alliances. The British fed their imaginations and fears with stories of planned German invasions in force—the bolt from the blue striking at London via the improbable surroundings of Esher or Dorking.[1] The French looked for the gap in the Vosges and the veiled figure of Strasbourg in the Place de la République. The Germans calculated timetables and peopled the woods that lay between the Masurian lakes with marauding Cossacks. It is in the nature of General Staffs to be alarmist; their alarmism fed on the increased military budgets of 1912–13. What they were afraid of generally was surprise. Given due warning and no politically inspired interference, they thought they could cope. Only the German General Staff were really apprehensive; hence the Schlieffen Plan and the agony which led the younger Moltke to mishandle it and so to make possible the miracle of the Marne.

Between the wars, however, despair or at least despondency to the point of defeatism was common to the General Staffs at least of three of the four powers who were to find themselves at war in September 1939. A profound spirit of pessimism, no matter how they sought to disguise it from these civilian lords and masters, gripped their commanders and chiefs of staff. It was so profound as to constitute an important common factor in the disintegration of the European political society in the 1930s, the second—for many of them the third—in their own lifetimes.

In parenthesis it must be remarked that this feeling of *déjà vu* is something which historians of the 1930s and of the origins of the Second World War fail almost entirely to mention. Yet they write of a generation in power which was composed almost entirely of victims of the First World War, whose memories, not only of the miseries of the war itself, but of the days which led to its opening and of the European collapse which followed its end, had been kept alive by twenty years of ubiquitous war memorials to the fallen, of two-minute silences on Armistice Day, poppies and Laurence Binyon or his analogues.

In part this professional pessimism came from the profound psychological shock administered to the self-esteem of the military in all countries by the failure of the First World War. To men whose entire professional ethos was that they were the élite of Europe as of their nation, chosen and anointed to lead their armies to victory, the failures of courage and doctrine, followed by the destruction by defeat of the framework of their previous certainties, made a new, revived optimism possible only through the surrender of some part of their professional personality and judgement to the charisma of a Hitler. That this was not common among the German staff corps can be seen in the contemptuous epithets of *Gummilöwe* (rubber lion) or *Lakaitel* (lackey) bestowed on von Blomberg and Keitel, Hitler's men, by their contemporaries.

This pessimism had equally deep roots, however, in the professional military distrust of the Covenant of the League of Nations. Article 16 proposed to maintain peace by threatening potential aggressors with economic or military sanctions, imposing on its signatories what the British Board of the Admiralty, in their comments of 3 July 1923 on the draft Treaty of Mutual Guarantee, called 'large and unknown commitments'.[2] Such open-ended commitments would logically 'necessitate an increase' in the forces of the signatories: 'Provision would have to be made for meeting their commitments under the Treaty as these commitments might arise when the services of the Fleet were required elsewhere...' But in fact the existence of these provisions of Article 16 were used to suggest a reduction in armaments. And against disarmament the professional military advisers of all countries found themselves in agreed opposition. 'European peace', wrote General Weygand in 1928, 'should continue to rest on the sanction of preponderant forces.'[3]

The professional military advisers had, after all, to cope with a degree of reduction in armaments which went well below what their professional instincts regarded as the bare minimum, but which was imposed on their countries by the economic uncertainties of the inter-war years and the increased demands made on the taxable capacity of their countries by the new areas of social expenditure into which the various European governments were increasingly being drawn. The economies which were forced on them, the run down of stores, the inability to replace obsolescent weapons, manoeuvres with hand-flags and dummy weapons, the axing of units, premature retirement of comrades, scrapping of warships, lent an autumnal melancholy to every phase of their professional lives.

Worst of all, however, was their professional feeling that the new League of Nations concealed a desperate loss of security. For the French General Staff, deprived both of a separate Rhineland and of the Anglo-American alliance, there was the contemplation of an imbalance of force and industrial potential already weighted against France and swinging steadily in Germany's favour. For the British General Staff and the Board of Admiralty there was the growth of Soviet pressure on Afghanistan, Persia and India and the increasing threat from Japan on the one hand and the continuous American demand for parity at a level which suited the Congressional requirements of the US Navy rather than the strategic needs of the Empire on the other. For the German General Staff, now concealed behind the modest title of the *Truppenamt*, there was the impossible task of defending Germany's eastern and western frontiers against France and Poland with an army of 100,000 men, a rag, tag and bobtail of Home Guards, *Freikorps*, SA, etc. and no air force. There was a strong element of make-believe in both manoeuvres and military planning in all the major powers, save only in Italy where, secure in Mussolini's hymning of their praises, the Italian generals gave up any serious military responsibilities entirely.

These feelings of insecurity were greatly increased after 1931. The British Chiefs of Staff had seen their military expenditures limited by the original Ten Years Rule in 1919. The provision that no war could be expected for ten years had been reiterated in the years 1925-7 for each of the services. In 1928 Winston Churchill had made it a revolving provision. In 1931 despite the protests of the Chiefs of Staff, military expenditure had been cut still more drastically to balance the crisis budget of the autumn when Britain went off gold. The Japanese attack in Manchuria in September 1931 and the activities of the Japanese naval landing party in its conflict with the Nineteenth Chinese Route Army in Shanghai in February 1932 had confronted the British Chiefs of Staff with a situation in which 'the whole of our territory in the Far East', as they reported to the Committee of Imperial Defence that same month,[4] 'as well as the coastline of India and the Dominions and our vast trade and shipping lies open to attack...' The Ten Years Rule was abolished. But the services were warned that the 'very serious financial and economic situation... would not justify an expanding expenditure by the Defence Services.'[5]

To the Japanese threat in the Far East was added, in January 1933, the appointment of Adolf Hitler as German Chancellor. His acceleration of the clandestine rearmament of Germany, especially in the air, quickly became known to the British and French, whose sources of information on the previous level of German armament were remarkably full, even, in the French case, to the point of considerable exaggeration. There was a joint Anglo-French *démarche* in Berlin in the summer of 1933,[6] and the revision of Macdonald's disarmament proposals of March 1933, put forward by Sir John Simon in September, was directly justified by the increasing disquiet which Hitler's actions in this field and against Austria had occasioned. Hitler's reply was to withdraw both from the League and Disarmament Conference. British negotiators attempted to reach a *modus vivendi* in the winter of 1933–4, and Hitler threw in his morsel of spurious reasonableness in the form of a proposal for a 300,000-man army. But the publication early in April 1934 of the new German defence budget which included sizeable open increases in expenditure gave the Doumergue–Barthou Government of National Concentration in France the opportunity to denounce all further discussions on disarmament in its Note of 17 April 1934.[7]

What made the French government's gesture so extraordinary was that instead of accompanying it with a programme of re-armament for the French armed forces, it cut French defence expenditure still further. The vigour of the government was put into Barthou's search for military allies, in the Soviet Union and in Italy, a search continued by Laval after Barthou's assassination. French strategy remained unchanged in its major essentials, though there was a small but significant change in the rate at which the frontier fortifications were being prepared and in the attitude of the High Command to the defence of the northern frontier. To understand the change it is necessary to go back a bit to the debate on the Maginot Line.

This vital debate on the report of the Commission on the Defence of the Frontiers took place before the Conseil supérieure de la Guerre on 17 December 1926 and 18 January 1927.[8] I described in an earlier chapter the considerations that had lead the Commission to propose a fortification of France's frontiers: the expected decline in the French birthrate, the belief that the lessons of 1914–18 pointed to the superiority of fire-power on the battlefield, and the necessity of preventing a second invasion and capture of France's richest industrial areas, lying as they do so close to the frontiers. To these points were added, in the minds of the assembled generals and politicians, the knowledge that under the terms of the Treaty of Locarno the Rhineland was due to be evacuated by 1930.

France's frontiers left six classic invasion routes open. In the south lay the Belfort gap. The frontier was then covered both by the Rhine and the Vosges up to the Lauter tributary of the Rhine at the point where the Rhine ceased itself to be the frontier, where a second route lay from Landau across to Haguenau. A third route lay through Saarbrücken towards Metz, a fourth down the Moselle valley through Luxembourg towards Metz or Montmédy. The heavily wooded Eifel and

Ardennes area and inundations along the Meuse intervened to separate the route to Metz from that down the Sambre and the Saillant de Chinay towards le Cateau and the Oise. A fifth route lay down and across the Escaut towards Béthune, Douai and Lens and the sixth struck down the coast of Flanders past Hazebrouck.[9]

The key to all this was the gap between the Vosges and the Ardennes, in which lay Metz. In the famous words of Vauban to Louis XIV: 'Les places fortes de votre Majesté défendent chacune une province. Metz défend l'Etat.'[10] Here, it was decided, the fortifications would be given all possible priority. Here they would be the strongest. The north was more difficult. From the Ardennes to the sea the frontier lay not with Germany but with Belgium, France's ally. To fortify the frontier would be to range heavy guns on the territory of France's ally, and to indicate to that ally that it had been written off by the French High Command. The question was really how to enter Belgium, as in 1914, to reinforce the Belgian line of frontier fortifications, or whatever line could be held against German attack behind the frontier. On that line battle would be joined. Although both Pétain and Foch assumed that French forces would enter Belgium whatever the Belgian attitude, Poincaré, then President of the Council, pointed out the impossibility of entering if the Belgians did not wish it.[11] What should then be done? The battlefield would have to be organised on the French frontier. In any case, since the battle was to be defensive on the French side, great quantities of mobile field fortifications material, *parcs mobiles*, would be required. In the meantime the length of the northern frontier requiring defence was to be effectively reduced by an extensive system of inundations and—this being a later addition[12]—by the development of certain fortified areas and lines of concrete field fortifications. It was the latter that the French turned to on Hitler's advent to power.

And it was at this point that budgetary considerations inter-vened to make these fortified areas mere empty shells of what was originally planned.

The years 1934–6 were disastrous for France. In Britain these were the years of the Defence Requirements Committee, the years in which the rearmament programme was debated, radar embarked upon, the Spitfire and Hurricane adopted, specifications issued for a strategic bomber type. No comparable developments can be seen in France. The tentative discussions of a rearmament effort were hamstrung by the weakness of the Flandin and Laval Governments, and even the moneys voted could not be spent, owing to the bad organisation of the supply side of the French War Ministry and the desuetude which had overtaken the French armaments industry in the 1920s.[13] In 1934 Schneider Creusot's machine tools were over twenty years old. Prototypes were developed but not decided upon, even though discussions of frontier defence assumed the presence of the weapons in large numbers. The 47 mm anti-tank gun was a case in point. It took from 1934 to 1937 to authorise develop-ment from a prototype because of a dispute over whether it should be regarded as an infantry or an artillery weapon. In the end the units had to make do with the 25 mm gun, the inadequacies of which were abundantly displayed in 1940. The French B1 *bis* heavy tank was excellent and could be produced at a rate of two to four a day. But there were seventeen different engines developed for it, none of them in mass production.[14]

The French were relying as usual on diplomacy rather than military power. In 1935 staff arrangements were reached with the Italians by which a French army corps fought on a putative Italo–Yugoslav front against a German invasion of Austria.[15] The break-up of the Stresa front on the Ethiopian issue made this a dead letter within months of its signature. The Franco–Soviet Pact of 1935 linked the French army with that of the

Soviets, which the French distrusted and still assessed by its defeat at Polish hands in the battle of Warsaw. On 6 March the Belgians denounced their alliance with France, choosing in September 1936 a position of neutralism. On 7 March 1936 Hitler's troops marched into the Rhineland.

The military reaction to this was to reiterate and reinforce the doctrine of the defensive, creating 'l'ossature permanente d'un champ de bataille',[16] by the construction of field works, barbed wire and anti-tank obstacles guarded by concrete pill boxes armed with machine-guns and, in particularly important sectors, casements for the famous French 75 mm, *fortification de campagne durable*, permanent field fortifications. The aim was to fill in all the *lacunae* in the existing fortifications, strengthen the continuous front on which all troops were placed. The speed of German rearmament, said General Weygand, did not permit anything revolutionary. Moreover, these permanent field fortifications were a lot cheaper than the enormous emplacements of the Maginot Line proper.

The French Military Intelligence was, in fact, grossly, almost grotesquely overestimating the strength of the German armed forces and its rate of development. In 1935 it estimated the effective strength of the German armed forces at about double the real figure: 700,000 as against 350,000, most of whom were new recruits. Their sudden absorbtion made the old Seeckt army of 100,000 disappear almost entirely into training *cadres*.[17] A year after the SA purge, the SA strength was being reckoned as the equivalent of sixty reserve divisions, an estimate which was almost total nonsense, considering the obliteration of the SA leadership by the 1934 murders. Five divisions of frontier police, which were para-military forces, armed with light weapons and under military discipline, had been identified. What French Intelligence did not allow for was that, barring the 15,000 men in the Rhineland, all these frontier police were incorporated into the *Wehrmacht* by the decree announcing German rearmament, so that French intelligence was counting them twice. As for the tanks and motorised infantry necessary for the *attaque brusquée* so greatly feared by French observers, they were only beginning to come into production.

This overestimation was to be continued throughout the years after 1935. In 1936 French estimates gave 295,000 Germans under arms in the Rhineland at the moment of re-militarisation,[18] a figure only obtained by counting the 150,000 members of the NSKK, the Nazi equivalent of the AA and RAC. A true figure would have been about 30,000, including the 15,000 of the *Landespolizei*. In 1938 Intelligence reported the Siegfried Line completed and manned with more divisions than were in the whole German army.

What was even more curious was that while every French military commentator made much of the terrors of the German *attaque brusquée* and a need for ever increasing armaments to match it, there was never any suggestion that perhaps its techniques ought to be adopted by the French army. A prototype French dive-bomber was examined and rejected. Light tanks were projected—and ultra heavy ones—but nothing was done to form them into whole Panzer divisions. Instead the French army huddled ever more closely into its fortifications. In October 1932 it was planning to occupy the Saar and seize part of the Rhineland as a negotiating factor in the event of any German breach of Locarno.[19] In March 1936 it turned out that nothing could be done without general mobilisation, and that only the most preliminary examination of the possibilities had been carried out.[20] Any action would take eight days to set into operation. Even the most small-scale of operations required full mobilisation. The *levée en masse* theory of warfare had imposed on the French Government and High Command much the same dilemma as bedevilled American defence policy before Macnamara's reforms. It had eliminated any chance of graduated deterrence, since it admitted only general war as the alternative to peace.

Thus the French army was huddled into its fortifications and pill boxes, determined to await the German offensive, still believing, despite everything, that its continuous line could be held against German armoured attack, a belief which bore an ever-decreasing relationship to the arms and weapons their units actually had as opposed to those on the drawing board, in prototype state or awaiting adoption. French military thinking was overloaded with Skybolts.

The British situation was profoundly different from that of France. French military thought was obsessed with the single, potentially more powerful enemy. British thinking, by contrast, was distracted, literally, by commitments all over the world. In 1937 Sir Thomas Inskip, then Minister for the Co-ordination of Defence defined Britain's defence tasks under four heads:[21] the defence of Great Britain; the defence of Britain's trade routes; the defence of British and Commonwealth overseas territory; and the defence of the territories of their allies. These commitments were recognised in 1919. Indeed, the Admiralty representative had faced severe criticism at the Imperial War Conference in 1917 for the manner in which Australia and New Zealand had been left defenceless against the marauding of Admiral von Hipper's squadron in the Pacific.[22] In the 1920s the commitments involved the protection of Australia, New Zealand and Malaya against possible Japanese pressure—primarily a navy responsibility; the protection of India against possible Soviet military pressure on Afghanistan and incitement of the North-West Frontier tribes; even protection of Canada against the United States.

The Canadian problem only came up briefly, during the

period of maximum pressure on Britain of the American 1916 and 1918 naval construction programmes when the decision was taken to lay down four super-battleships, the super-Hoods as they were known. At the time the Admiralty representative saw the problem entirely in terms of protecting the Canadian grain trade.[23] Otherwise the defence of Canada against its over-mighty neighbour to the south was left to the fertile imagination of the Canadian Director of Military Operations and Intelligence, Colonel J. Sutherland ('Buster') Brown, whose conviction of the inevitability of war with the United States, unshared by any other member of the Canadian Defence Establishment, led him to draft Defence Scheme No. 1. This envisaged a grandiose invasion of the United States across the 49th Parallel, occupying Spokane, Seattle, Portland, converging towards Fargo in North Dakota and continuing in the general direction of Minneapolis: not bad for a militia of 38,000 whose budget in 1921–2 permitted a full nine days' training that year.[24]

The brunt of the strategic planning prior to 1931 was inevitably borne by the Royal Navy. The Washington Treaties of 1922 had ended the Anglo–Japanese alliance, prohibited any new fortifications in the area lying between Singapore, Hawaii and the Japanese Home Islands, and put an effective limitation on the navy's capital ships and aircraft carriers which established on paper parity with the United States and an actual two-power standard as against Japan and France, at least so far as capital ships were concerned. The strategy evolved to cope with the navy's responsibilities divided the battle fleet between home and Mediterranean waters, envisaging the dispatch of the bulk of the Mediterranean fleet via Suez to Singapore in the event of Japanese belligerency. The manoeuvre was planned but never executed, although the concentration of cruisers (some carrying troops) on Shanghai in 1927 afforded a kind of low-level demonstration of its possibilities. But the commitment (and the development of Singapore) remained unchallenged until 1939, though by 1935–6 it was clear that the cost of maintaining and providing replacements for a fleet capable of matching that of Japan in the Far East and of maintaining naval supremacy in European waters was beyond Britain's financial capacity.[25]

To the defence of the Empire was added in 1925 the military responsibilities of guaranteeing the Locarno Settlement. In the 1920s very little notice was taken of these in military terms. They remained a kind of solemn shibboleth to be produced whenever the Chiefs of Staff were required to report generally on Britain's military position. Since the guarantee had been given formally to all three of the States whose frontiers had been guaranteed, any serious military planning was out of the question. What Locarno did do was to focus the attention of the Army on the possibility of involvement in another large-scale war on the Continent—the ultimate form of land-war in which the army would return to the position of dominance over its sister-services it had occupied in 1916–18.

The matter was of importance because of the growing body of opinion, led by Captain Liddell Hart's writings, that the commitment to send the BEF to France in 1914 had constituted a disastrous abandonment of Britain's previous wartime policy of using her maritime supremacy to lure and extend her Continental enemies until their over-extensions and exhaustion made them vulnerable to the final *coup de grâce* from Britain and her allies. Nowhere did this doctrine strike stronger hold than in the Treasury.[26]

Hitler's advent coincided with the beginnings of economic recovery in Britain. For the 1934–5 financial year a smallish surplus was anticipated, allowing the services the chance to repair some of the deficiencies which the desperate need for a balanced budget had imposed on them in 1931–5, and which had led them to warn openly that they could no longer guarantee the security of the Empire. It would have been adequate if the services had simply been given some guide as to how much extra funding they could expect and left to produce their own increased estimates. It was the Treasury—or rather Sir Warren Fisher who hit on the device of an interdepartmental Cabinet committee, to make a common recommendation. The Defence Requirements Committee, consisting of himself, Sir Maurice Hankey, Sir Robert Vansittart and the three Chiefs of Staff was to be the result.[27] Sir Warren's Germanophobia was only matched by that of Sir Robert Vansittart, and his long-standing campaign to make the Civil Service function as an entity had, in defence matters, been thwarted previously by the doctrinal differences between Lord Trenchard and his army and navy colleagues.

It was the combination of Fisher and Vansittart which forced the DRC to look beyond the menace of Japan to Germany and pronounce her the ultimate potential enemy against whom long-range defence policy must be planned. This same combination urged that Britain's 'subservience' to America, on whom no reliance whatever could be placed, should be abandoned and the most strenuous efforts made to reach agreement with Japan.[28] This latter view failed to command the support either of the Foreign Office or the Cabinet. Its enunciation clashed with the pronouncement of the Amau doctrine and the revelation of Japanese determination to be free of the restrictions of the Washington and London Naval Treaties. Instead, the long effort to 'educate' American opinion in the realities of the world situation and the need for common action in the Far East was embarked upon. It was to be some time before it appeared to be reaping any benefits.

Both army and air force were encouraged by the setting up of the DRC to think in terms of an expeditionary force with a sizeable air component. It was to prove a vain hope. The DRC report was referred to a ministerial committee. From this it re-emerged in June 1934.[29] It was again the Treasury, speaking through the mouth of the Chancellor, Neville Chamberlain, which made the three vital points which were to affect British strategy. Financial weakness and the need for financial recovery meant that management would have to proceed on a basis of priorities. Priority would have to be given to the defence of Great Britain rather than to the Far East. The chief danger Britain faced was in the air. Thus the RAF would have its allocation increased but this would be firmly tied to the development of Britain's air defences. The navy's hopes of a new two-power standard were dismissed. The army could only look to a BEF as a second line, a long-term development. The six divisions of the original DRC were simply out. In accordance with this view, a Belgian request for a 'preventative guarantee' of her territory was turned down as 'inopportune'.[30] And the army's request for £40 million was cut by over half.

The Chiefs of Staff and their ministers naturally let out a howl of protest. Their estimates of German strength were at this time inflated though not as much as those of the French, giving the Germans 21 infantry, 3 cavalry divisions, and 2 mechanised divisions in process of formation.[31] Their figures of German rearmament in the air were more accurate. The public attack on them by Mr Churchill and others, using more exaggerated figures almost certainly supplied, for reasons that remain unclear, from official German as well as Nazi sources, led to two revised air programmes. The DRC was reconstituted and reported in July and again in November 1935.[32] The most remarkable element in its report was its selection of 1939 as the date beyond which it would not be safe to postpone an

effective state of preparedness. The second was its stern underlining of the impossibility of coping with three enemies at
once: 'A cardinal requirement of our national and imperial
security is that our foreign policy should be so conducted as to
avoid the possibility of developing of a situation in which we
might be confronted simultaneously with the hostility, open
or veiled, of Japan in the Far East, Germany in the west and
any Power on the main lines of communication between the
two.' For, by November 1935, the Ethiopian affair had lined
Britain and Italy firmly against each other.

Once more the DRC trotted out the need for an expeditionary force, now called the Field Force, for use in Europe,
of five divisions, with provision for reinforcement with
twelve Territorial divisions over the first eight months of
hostilities. Once more it became clear that ministers were far
from happy about a major commitment to a Continental war.
Expenditure on the Territorial divisions was postponed for
three years. And when the Rhineland crisis of March 1936
necessitated a promise of staff talks with the French and Belgians, all that Britain could offer were two regular divisions
ninety days after the outbreak of hostilities and then only on a
basis of 'perhaps'.[33]

It was only at this date, March 1936, that the official rearmament of Britain as opposed to the repair of deficiencies
began. And it began on the basis of an army the commitment
of which to a European campaign was for three years given the
lowest of all priorities by the majority of the Cabinet. The
third DRC report recommended that the Field Force should
be available within a fortnight of the outbreak of war. By
December 1936 the Chancellor was already worried by the
manpower implication of sending seventeen divisions overseas,
was arguing that a large air force would be more of a deterrent
than a larger army and was pleading the danger from public

opinion if commitment to a major Continental campaign seemed to be under preparation in peacetime. In March 1937 the Treasury realised that the estimates of the three services were already escalating alarmingly. The Chiefs of Staff were still pressing for a limited Continental army of seventeen divisions. But in May the Chancellor, Chamberlain, became Premier, and the matter was again referred to a committee. That committee already had other matters on its mind. One of them was the Admiralty's continuing demand for a genuine two-power standard. And its members were also immensely concerned with Britain's vulnerability from the air, the spectre of a 'knock-out blow from the air' which, with the so-called 'Ideal Scheme' of air defence, was currently being considered by the Committee of Imperial Defence.[34] The 'Ideal Scheme,' it turned out, would absorb two of the twelve planned Territorial divisions. Its cost would greatly inflate the Army Estimates. By December 1937 the position was so bad that Sir Thomas Inskip was induced to draw up the memorandum already cited which put the defence of the territories of Britain's allies fourth on the list of priorities, with the ruling that for the time being no provision could be made for this; the primary role of the army became 'the defence of imperial commitments, including anti-aircraft defence at home'.

Thus was enunciated the notion of a war of limited liability, to be fought in defence of imperial commitments, on a scale of intensity less than that to be expected in operations against Germany on the Continent. Strategic commentators played with the idea of a small armoured corps of two élite divisions for Continental commitments.[35] But the truth was that the armed forces were locked up in Egypt and Palestine, facing the Arab revolt and a steady build up of Italian troops in Libya.[36] For, by the summer of 1937 Anglo–Italian relations had deteriorated to the point where the possibility of war had reluctantly to be faced by the military planners. When an Italian submarine attacked a British destroyer on the Spanish non-intervention patrol, war came very close indeed. In February 1938 the proposals for the Field Force were consequently revised to provide four infantry divisions and one mobile division, to be ready within two months of the outbreak of war 'in an Eastern theatre': two more divisions were to be ready after four months.[37] Nothing more would be available until the eighth month at the earliest. Even these proposals were subject to Cabinet reduction.

At that moment two and a half infantry divisions or their equivalent were engaged in colonial garrison duties. A mobile division was in process of being organised in Egypt. The Indian Government was committed to providing three brigade groups for overseas service, one for Egypt and Aden, one for Singapore and one to protect the Persian oil fields. There were 57,000 British troops in India.

In March 1938, the Germans marched into Austria. British intelligence reported that the German army could put one hundred infantry and four to six armoured divisions into the field in the event of war—a considerable exaggeration.[38] At the end of April 1938 the French ministers Daladier and Bonnet appeared in London pressing for staff talks in view of the obvious prospects of a German–Czechoslovak conflict. They ran into very deep misgivings on the part of the Chiefs of Staff. This is hardly surprising, since the best that could be done was to provide the first echelon of the Field Force, two divisions with an incomplete quota of Corps troops and many deficiencies in equipment. Nothing more could be provided for a year or more after the outbreak of hostilities. Indeed, in Mr Chamberlain's view, the only reason for their dispatch was to protect the Advanced Air Striking Force.[39]

To such a pitch had the financial and strategic anxieties of

Britain brought her that in military terms she had practically deserted the European mainland entirely. The army was only prepared for a war in an eastern theatre. The navy was committed to blockade but also to a major transfer of forces to Far Eastern waters in the event of a Japanese threat to Singapore or Australia. Secret Anglo–American staff talks on future action against Japan in fact took place in January 1938 in London.[40] The major part of Britain's armed forces was tied down in Palestine and the Middle East on the imperial lines of communication. Militarily, Britain had virtually abandoned Europe and the stability of the European system—a fact of which Hitler's address to his generals on Guy Fawkes Day 1937, the Hossbach Conference, shows him to have been well aware. Politically, however, Britain remained part of the European system.[41] In only five months, Britain was pressing France for staff talks. In seventeen months Britain was at war. How this came about is a matter of politics rather than strategy. It did little to reduce the incidence of military pessimism.

Certainty of British involvement, moral certainty, was the principal cause of military pessimism for Germany. The German armed forces had spent the 1920s gloomily confronting their almost total inability to guarantee the defence of their country against France and her Polish and Czech allies. The German navy seriously wondered whether it was worth making any plans for war in the North Sea with the apparent impossibility of stopping any French offensive west of the Elbe. Retreat behind the Skagerrak and Kattegat and the sealing off of the Baltic appeared all that could be hoped for.[42] Seen through the eyes of the *Truppenamt*, the *Einwohnerwehren* and the political para-military forces seemed only of the most limited military usefulness, units whose sacrifice might give a little more time for the preparation of defences deeper within Germany.[43] Mobilisation plans were exercises, no more. In 1931, at a time of great tension with Poland, the best that could be planned was to use German superiority at sea to cut the enemy off from the sea and destroy the coastal fortifications of Gdynia.[44]

On his advent to power Hitler ordered a rearmament programme to be completed by 1938[45] and announced his intention of making an agreement with Britain.[46] The news was greatly comforting to his hearers. His wilder ravings about *Lebensraum* were at first simply dismissed by his hearers as typical political ramblings. His adventurousness, on the other hand, they found alarming.

The depth of their anxieties can be inferred from the orders issued by General von Blomberg on 25 October 1933 on the occasion of German withdrawal from the League.[47] The strictest secrecy was enjoined. Military sanctions from France, Belgium, Poland and Czechoslovakia were feared. Any attack on German shipping, and any entry on sovereign German territory was to be met with armed resistance on the spot without reference to chances of military success. In May 1934, he ordered that in the event of enemy action against the Rhineland the frontier forces were to be strengthened by bringing in the SA.[48] The purge of the SA leadership in June 1934 made the proposal useless. By October 1934 the institution of military sanctions by France was recognised as a *casus belli*.[49] The signature of the German–Polish Non-Aggression Pact in January 1934 had greatly relieved the military planners' fears of a new two-front war. But the intention of the 1933 orders to treat any military sanctions against Germany as war was underlined when the decision was taken on 12 March 1935 to reissue the orders of October 1933 under the title 'Instructions for the first phase of Command in War'.[50]

By March 1935, however, the political situation had worsened. The presuppositions as outlined by General von Reichenau[51] were: a Franco–Italian decision to attack Germany, a Czech mobilisation, Russian air force plans to use Czech bases against Germany, British and Belgian neutrality. Von Reichenau envisaged a French invasion of the Rhineland, Italian invasion of Austria to be met by the holding of the Roer–Rhine–Black Forest line, and a sudden attack on Czechoslovakia, once her attitude was clear, to deny Russia the air bases. It was in pursuit of this latter idea that von Blomberg on 2 May 1935 ordered the study of a sudden attack on an unnamed south-east state 'without reference to the unsatisfactory state of our armaments at the moment'. The subsequent fate of this order to which the code name *Schulung* was given is difficult to trace.[52] Some of it must have occupied the General Staff, as a year later von Blomberg issued an order rebuking staff officers for careless talk on the subject of military preparations against Czechoslovakia.[53] The date of the *Schulung* order is significant: it was the date of the signature of the Russo–Czechoslovak Pact, complementary to the Franco–Soviet Pact.

Orders for the year 1935–6 were, in fact, issued in July 1935 to cover the defence of the western frontiers of Germany. They have not survived; but it is clear from the orders issued at the time of the reoccupation of the Rhineland that they covered the same ground as the 1933 orders.[54] The Rhine was to be held by the armed *Landespolizei* against all attempts to cross it. All bridges and all floating craft on the Rhine were to be destroyed. The fall-back position lay in the Black Forest area.

The decision to reoccupy the Rhineland was taken by Hitler in the course of February 1936. Two sets of considerations appear to have governed his timing. The first was the clear evidence that Mussolini, one of the two guarantors of Locarno, was threatening to denounce it, if France agreed to apply oil sanctions against him. The other was an instinct that the Ethiopian conflict was nearing its end, and that if he did not act soon, the chance of profiting from the disarray into which it had thrown the Stresa front would be lost. The manoeuvre was brilliantly executed on the political front. In all only fifteen battalions were used actually to enter the Rhineland and only three of these, reinforced with tanks and armoured cars, actually crossed the Rhine. Behind them, however, the bulk of the new German army, thirteen infantry divisions divided into three army commands, with the main weight, eight divisions in all in the south, was made ready. The advance troops were under instruction to occupy prepared fortifications—*Sperrzone*—and to halt the enemy advance. In general, an invasion of German territory was to be treated as before, as war.

In the event, as noticed earlier, the action passed off without any French or British reaction. The Anglo–French staff talks of April 1936 caused some political alarm and the German Foreign Ministry gave wide circulation to a speech in the Commons by Lloyd George. But the German military and naval attachés in London, Colonel (later General) Geyr von Schweppenberg and Captain Wassner, were able to report in detail on the very limited availability of British forces. The provisional war instructions for the German navy issued on 27 May 1936,[55] therefore, specifically left war with Britain out of consideration as 'Such a war', in the drafting officer's words, 'would have to be conducted under special conditions and in such a case no war instructions looking to a successful termination of the war could be issued in advance.' The 'normal case' was therefore taken, a war on two fronts with France, Russia, Lithuania, Czechoslovakia and possibly Poland. Italy's attitude, according to the navy, had no influence on the war order. The neutrality of Britain, the Netherlands, the United States and Japan was, however, all-important.

That summer the commanders' war games, as noticed

above, again involved the question of a strategic pre-emptive strike against Czechoslovakia. That it was still only a matter of staff studies is shown by von Blomberg's rebuke of those who had made it the subject of war games and exercises at a lower level.

In the meantime, however, the key word was 'quiet'. The German Foreign Minister told the American Ambassador to Moscow, William Bullitt, that until the new western fortifications were completed Germany would keep her head down.[56] So in fact she did, the only military involvement being the dispatch of the Condor legion to Spain. Hitler in the meantime had embarked on a major effort to use the Spanish Civil War to create an anti-Soviet front. The anti-Comintern pact and the Axis were the general outcome. The sincerity of the policy can be seen in the secret memorandum with which he launched the second round of rearmament, the Four Year Plan.[57] This memorandum drafted in August 1936 after prolonged rows with Schacht, who regarded any further rearmament as likely to prove disastrous to the German economy, was predicated as the belief that war with Russia was inevitable. The economy —and the armed forces—were given four years to be ready for war.

In the summer of 1937, *Reichskriegsminister* von Blomberg, now Field Marshal, issued new military orders for the year 1937–8.[58] The general section with which these orders opened noted that no danger of aggression against Germany existed at that moment. No power wanted war, and the deficiencies in their preparations for war, 'in particular those of Russia', von Blomberg gave as the grounds for this so very definite statement. Continuous preparations for war were, however, necessary in order to counter attacks at any time 'to enable the military exploitation of politically favourable opportunities should they occur'. Plans were to be drafted for the probable course of military action in the event of war with France, Russia and Czechoslovakia. Case Red covered attack in the west, defence in the east; and Case Green, attack in Czechoslovakia and defence in the west.

German military intelligence, it should be noted, was no better at assessing the plans of potential enemies than were the intelligence services in France and Britain. In the case of war, the instructions noted: 'The opening of the war will probably be accompanied by an all-out attack by the French army and air force...' Hardly could the drafter have displayed his total ignorance of French military theory and plans more convincingly. The political provisos were British neutrality. British participation, the memorandum noted, would result in 'our military position being worsened to an unbearable, even hopeless, state'. These orders, it must be emphasised, were directed eventually at the General Staff. They involved general preparations, preparations for the two most likely eventualities, Case Red and Case Green, and staff studies pure and simple for the special cases: Otto (a *coup de main* against Austria), Richard (war with Republican Spain), and Enlargement Red/Green, the addition of Britain, Poland or Lithuania to the enemies envisaged in Red and Green. Although they envisaged possible aggressive action, they did not include any time or date. The row which followed their issue, to which I referred earlier, was part of the on-going struggle between the Chief of Staff to the Army and the War Ministry on the matter of responsibility.

Hitler's Hossbach address was, however, to confine this struggle to the archives. For the first time a timetable was mentioned, even if in the vaguest of terms. It was this which upset the military men, von Blomberg and Fritsch, and the Foreign Minister, Baron von Neurath, so much as to cause Fritsch to ask if he ought to cancel his leave, and determine Hitler to be rid of them as soon as possible. The rest of the speech they had heard before, *ad nauseam*, with one other exception—Hitler's characterisation of Britain as a hate-crazed antagonist. The prospect of war with Britain loomed menacingly on the horizon. Fritsch reiterated his fears of a French offensive in the Rhineland, the Siegfried Line being in his view of insignificant value. Von Blomberg characterised the German motorised divisions as still more or less incapable of movement. Raeder and von Neurath remained in appalled silence. Von Blomberg was, however, sufficiently moved to reverse the orders for Case Green a month later with an elaborate 'iffy' and 'butty' political introduction.[59] This had the effect of directing General Beck's attention to the real seriousness of Hitler's plans and suppositions. The stage was set for the long battle of the summer of 1938 which was to end with Beck's resignation and the Munich Conference, the triumph of radical nationalist politics over a military conservatism which was, as we shall see in the next chapter, to become steadily more 'European' in its concern.

5 Reluctant Warriors: European Chiefs of Staff and the Fear of War, 1938-1939

The European Chiefs of Staff had good reasons for the profound pessimism with which they regarded the prospects of war in 1938. In no case had the programmes of rearmament embarked on in the mid-1930s reached their positions of fulfilment. Fear of attack from the air, fear of a war on two fronts, fears of the new weapons added to the general unreadiness which sat so heavily on the shoulders and troubled the sleep of the Chiefs of Staff and their staffs of planners and intelligence advisers. But their fears were the stronger for being fitted into a framework of thought about the nature of modern war which encompassed a much wider circle of official advisers in the various European governments than the professional military. This framework of thought centred on the war potential of the various European nations—that is, on their relative capacity in terms of industrial strength, accessibility to raw materials, capacity for earning foreign exchange and mobilising foreign credit, trained industrial manpower and agricultural potential, in a word, a German word, *Wehrwirtschaft*.

The concept of *Wehrwirtschaft* was developed in Germany in the reflections of the German General Staff on the reasons for Germany's defeat in the 1914-18 war. Its arch-prophet was General Georg Thomas, who entered the Armaments Office, the *Hereswaffenamt* of the *Reichswehrministerium* in 1928, became its chief in 1933, and in 1934 became head of the newly created office for *Wehrwirtschaft und Waffenwesen* and remained Germany's leading expert in the field until his powers and office were swallowed up in Albert Speer's take-over of the Ministry for Armaments and Munitions in 1942.[1] He defined the field as including 'the measures for the technical economic preparation of the [nation's] economy for war and, as a preparation for that, the exercise of influence upon the peacetime economy in terms of armaments, by those responsible for national defence'.[2] In his view it also encompassed the 'study of the economic thoughts for war of one's own country and of other states, as well as the study of the interrelationships between the economy and the strength of the [nation's] military posture both in actual and in ideal terms.'[3] The definition betrays in its mixture of the intellectual and the pragmatic the philosophical idealism of the German and the practical training of the professional soldier.

The nearest British equivalent is the concept of 'economic warfare', one which seeps into the papers of the Committee of Imperial Defence in the mid-1930s without any philosophical discussion or trace of its authorship.[4] It too grew out of the experience of the Ministry for the Blockade in the First World War. It represented, however, the coming together of three different sets of developments. The first of these was the setting up in 1919, as a weak successor to the wartime Ministry of Blockade, of the Advisory Committee on Trade Questions in Time of War. It met very rarely in the 1920s but from 1935 its Sub-Committee on Economic Pressures was engaged in considering the question of economic sanctions against Italy in particular, and economic pressures in time of conflict in general.

The second development was the establishment in 1924 by the Committee of Imperial Defence (CID) of the Principal Supply Officers Committee, a standing committee consisting of the principal supply officers of the three armed services and a representative of the Board of Trade. The Committee's responsibilities were to ascertain and keep a watch on stocks of raw materials; to prepare a list of essential items and make arrangements to prohibit their export in time of war; to prepare plans for increased output; to maintain lists of contractors who could be called on in time of war; and to report periodically on all these matters to the main committees. The intention was to create what the official historians called 'a machinery and habit of constant and sympathetic consideration' of the problems of supply in wartime. The Committee was enlarged in 1927 by the inclusion of the Dominions High Commissioners and put under the direct chairmanship of the President of the Board of Trade.[5]

The third development took place in 1929 when the Cabinet and CID found themselves confronted with a number of reports, originally of French provenance, on 'industrial mobilisation' in time of war and on the interest shown in this subject in Germany. A small staff was brought together to study the matter in the winter of 1929–30, and from this came in 1931 the Industrial Intelligence Centre, set up by Major Desmond Morton, who had been seconded to the Board of Trade in 1929.[6] The Centre assumed a more overt role in 1935, being affiliated to the Department of Overseas Trade; but its reports continued to go directly to the CID.

The economic and financial disaster which overtook Britain in the summer and autumn of 1931 made the consideration of British economic strength absolutely central to the whole rearmament process as the debate on it unfolded from 1935 onwards.

The position of the United States was of key importance in this. Roosevelt's behaviour in 1933 had left much of the Cabinet, especially Neville Chamberlain, convinced that his administration neither understood nor cared what the effects of their policy of concentrating entirely on the domestic

economy of the United States were on world trade in general
and on Britain's economic position in particular.[7] The President's unwillingness to show any understanding of the effects
of American policy on Britain's capacity to service her war
debts to the United States (and, to judge by his private corre-
spondence, his total lack of comprehension of the issues)[8] was
followed by an equal unwillingness to moderate the effects of
his dear silver policy on China's economic capacity to stand up
to Japan in 1935. The Johnson Act of 1934, which barred
access to the American capital market to any state in default
on its existing obligations to the United States, and the
American neutrality legislation of 1935–6, faced the British
Government with the possibility that in a new war with Germany Britain would not only have to finance the war out of
her own resources but also act as the principal arsenal for
herself and her allies.

This prospect linked Britain's rearmament effort directly
with her economic strength and level of economic activity. In
1936 and early 1937 this was enough to sustain the level of
British rearmament, and it was only the escalating costs of the
programme itself which led the Treasury and the Minister for
the Co-ordination of Defence, Sir Thomas Inskip, to put on
the brakes. In his second report to the Cabinet of early
February 1938,[9] Inskip, for example, pointed out that the
service estimates seemed to be running at £2,000 million
instead of the £1,500 million originally envisaged. 'Nothing',
he wrote, 'operates more strongly to deter a political aggressor
from attacking this country than our [economic] stability. But
if other countries were to detect serious signs of strain, the
deterrent would at once be lost.' Given the current existing
favourable conditions of trade, the Treasury, he reported, felt
Britain could finance a five-year defence programme of £1,650
million. But, he continued, the plain facts were that 'it is

beyond the resources of this country to make proper provision in peace for the defence of the British Empire against three major powers in three different theatres of war'. The Chancellor, Sir John Simon, in the Cabinet discussion of this report, added that the figure of £1,650 million 'not only placed a terrible strain on the national finances but could not be increased without financial disorganisation to an extent which might weaken this country'.[10]

The favourable terms of trade were not maintained. By November 1938, with the Roosevelt recession biting hard, Sir John Simon was protesting that the yield in revenue was 'sagging with the declining activity of the country as a whole. . . . In the end our monetary reserves which have already been heavily depleted since the [Munich] crisis by the withdrawal of foreign capital from this country would be still more rapidly exhausted and we should have lost the means of carrying on a long struggle altogether.'[11] Sir Warren Fisher had spelt out the British version of *Wehrwirtschaft* in his comments on Sir Thomas Inskip's first report in December 1937:[12]

A modern war is peoples at war and success means ensuring the maintenance of resources as well as their effective use . . . The Treasury is as much concerned with our military survival as are the military departments; without economic stability—which includes continued capacity to obtain necessities from abroad, the best use of manpower and the maximum industrial power—we shall be defeated.

The view taken by Inskip and Chamberlain as to the deterrent power of Britain's economic strength certainly held more than a grain of truth so far as the German military and industrial advisers to Hitler were concerned. Germany's foreign exchange earnings even in 1936 were less than adequate to cover the raw material import needs of the armaments industry and the gap between the consumption and production of food.

It was this situation which led the Economic Minister, Dr Schacht, *inter alia*, to urge a reduction in the pace of German rearmament and to embark on his own negotiations for a *détente* with the French Popular Front Government of Léon Blum.[13] This situation led to the setting up of the Four Year Plan. The experience of the first eighteen months of the Four Year Plan was by no means happy. The most rigid controls could not, for example, prevent a shortage of sheet steel from developing, which slowed down parts of the armament programme to a noticeable extent. The Hossbach Conference was, in fact, originally called to decide on priorities in the allocation of armour plate between the three armed services. Hitler's change of heart towards Britain is more than adequately illustrated by the fact that his decision awarded the priority to the navy. Schacht's increasing disagreements with Goering led to his resignation in November 1937. But even the deliberate avoidance of any armament in depth could not prevent the foreign exchange situation worsening, with consequent effects on the supply of food, steel, non-ferrous metals and oil. Even the *Wehrmacht* had to accept a considerable export activity by the very armaments industry whose products they most needed themselves. The position grew steadily worse throughout 1938, the Sudeten crisis and the general tensions of the year being reflected in a further increase in raw materials prices, especially non-ferrous metals.

It was this which led the economic advisers to the German Government to their last efforts early in 1939 to get Hitler to slow down the rate of rearming—but in vain. Schacht was removed from his remaining office. State Secretary Brinkmann retired with a bad nervous breakdown after a speech in Cologne in which he was reported to have said that Germany had exhausted her foreign reserves, emptied the state's coffers, reached the limits of taxable capacity and produced a demand

for manpower so acute that the quality of the work was simply
no longer reliable.[14] The Army General Staff, it emerges, were
grossly overestimating France's military and industrial potential. In the technical literature can be found statements to the
effect that (by contrast with Germany) France was largely
self-supporting in food. The French armaments industry was
described as being in its 'scope and productivity the strongest
in Europe'.[15] In modern warfare, it was said, each soldier under
arms needed seven to eight workers in industry to support him.
Thus an army of three million would need a labour force of
fifty-four million which, lacking any overseas credit, Germany
was quite incapable of providing. As for the *Blitzkrieg*, or
rather the short war, the General Staff's view was that this
false conception had already led once to Germany's ruin, in
1914. And it was an automatic assumption of virtually all
writers on *Wehrwirtschaft* in Germany that in the event of
war with Germany, Britain would again, as in 1914–18, be
able to rely on American industrial strength.

It is against this background that the pessimism of the
General Staffs in 1938 and 1939 must be considered. The
easiest to discuss are the Italians. The rigid separation between
the three armed services, the absence of anything resembling
a combined Chiefs of Staff machinery or a Ministry of Defence,
Mussolini's own complete lack of either staff or expertise,
meant that the approach of war in Europe found the Italian
armed forces militarily unprepared, without any plans save
theoretical staff exercises prepared by the staffs of the three
services virtually in a vacuum. Since there were no war plans,
there were no plans for industry. Mussolini himself seems to
have remained in the profoundest ignorance of all this, convinced by his own rhetoric that all was well with the forces of
the inheritor of the mantle of Pompey and Caesar.

This alone can explain the extraordinary ignorance he was

to display in the summer of 1939, having signed the Pact of Steel, the alliance with Germany in May 1939. In 1939, according to the Diaries of Count Ciano, his son-in-law, he had been reduced to instructing the Fascist prefects of each region to make a visual count of the aircraft on the military airfields in their regions as the only way of learning the real strength of the Italian Air Force.[16] Already in February 1939, Ciano was still recording Mussolini's total ignorance of what was going on in the army and air force.[17] The revelations of the unpreparedness of the Italian army for war, which Ciano unleashed on him in August 1939 to stop him rushing into war with France, came as a total surprise.[18] Yet the Italian military at least had been broadcasting their anxieties for well over a year. While Mussolini was carefully burying von Ribbentrop's request for an immediate German–Italian–Japanese alliance the previous October, General Pariani, the Chief of the Italian Army Staff, was expressing himself to the Germans on the need for German–Italian staff conversations in tones of near panic.[19] The possibility of war with France, let alone with Britain, had reduced him to a state of nerves so embarrassing to the German High Command that their military attaché in Rome had to be instructed to have nothing to do with him for the time being.[20]

The French army in 1938–9 displays a similar deterioration in morale, slower perhaps but none the less significant. Officially the French army leadership, especially General Gamelin, was always confident. They saw no reason to doubt the effectiveness of the defensive strategy they had adopted or their ability to go over to the offensive once the German attack had been defeated. Only in one area were France's defences insufficient. That was in the air. Pierre Cot, Air Minister in the Blum Government had agreed in October 1936 to an expansion of the French air force to 1,500 front-line machines over five years.[21] In 1937 this figure was cut to three years, but the record of the nationalised aircraft industry in 1937 was deplorable. In January 1938 Cot was succeeded as Air Minister by Guy la Chambre who introduced a target of 1,800 aircraft by 1 January 1939 rising to 2,600 by 1941 with one hundred per cent reserves. At the same time he put out the first feelers for a large-scale purchase of aircraft in America.[22] In the meantime, however, France was defenceless against air attack and the Air Staff insisted on the need to avoid war in 1938. On 15 March when M. Blum, once more Premier, asked the *Comité permanente de la défense nationale* to examine the case for intervention in Spain, the Chief of Air Staff, General Vuillemin, said that would mean the annihilation of his forces within a fortnight.[23] That same day, the *Comité* also considered how France could actively assist in the defence of Czechoslovakia. It emerged from the presentations by M. Daladier, then War Minister, backed by the Chiefs of Staff to the Army and the Air Force, that all France could do was to pin down a number of German divisions on the western frontier. A major offensive was simply excluded. It would run into the German frontier fortifications, the Siegfried Line, the state of completion of which French intelligence grossly overestimated.[24]

The matter was greatly complicated by Gamelin's unwillingness to say anything which might provide a handle for the politicians to use against the military. Thus, during the May weekend crisis of 1938, asked what France could do for Czechoslovakia, he replied 'I will attack', but warned that it could be 'a long and exacting battle'.[25] On 8 June he issued orders for a French attack on the Rhineland to be launched through the Saarland against the German defences; but his instruction that only a minimum number of troops were to be used makes it clear that what was envisaged was a reconnaissance in force.[26] Gamelin was, in fact, concerned that the French political leadership should be nudged into inactivity but not in such a way that they could put the blame on the army.

This can be seen in the careful discounting by him and his staff of the highly optimistic reports of the French military attaché in Moscow. In 1937 he even refused the Soviets permission to attend the French autumn manoeuvres.[27] In April 1938 he said he preferred Russian neutrality.[28] And in September he told Daladier that Russia could only be of secondary importance in the defence of Czechoslovakia.[29] French military intelligence paid especial attention to the effects of the purges on the Soviet military system. Their denigration of the Czech military in 1938, whom they had previously rated very highly, was the subject of bitter protest by General Faucher, the French military attaché in Prague, who subsequently renounced his French citizenship.[30] But the High Command had made the mistake of allowing him to remain in Prague for fifteen years, and regarded him as more Czech than French in his judgement.

The Air Staff's view was one of real panic. During the month of August, General Vuillemin made a week's official visit to Germany. He was shown the production rates in the German air industry, he was given a demonstration of dive-bombers in action, he was shown airfields carefully packed with aircraft, assembled each day from other fields to give him a vastly inflated figure of German air strength.[31] His own greatly exaggerated picture of the strength of the German air force was echoed by those of the famous American flyer, Colonel Charles Lindbergh, then resident in France.[32] The effect was to leave the French Air Staff with the feeling that their own aircraft were largely outclassed. On his return to Paris, General Vuillemin again told Daladier his air forces would be destroyed in the first fortnight of fighting. French insistence that there should be no air operations against German towns in general or against the Ruhr was directly bound up with the fear of reprisals. All the principal cities in northern France, including Paris, would have to be evacuated prior to a French offensive, so Gamelin told the British in September 1938.[33] Daladier left for Munich with General Vuillemin's parting words, that the French air force only had 700 front line planes, that their performance was *insuffisante*, and that 60 per cent would be lost in the first fortnight of war.[34]

After Munich the French military continued to show the utmost pessimism in its judgement of Hitler's future plans. The collapse of Czechoslovakia had ended their old reliance on an eastern front as a means of restraining Hitler. Gamelin tried instead a southern front. His memoranda of October 1938[35] looked to a strengthening of France's position with Spain on the one hand and Turkey and the Balkans on the other. Italy he considered a likely enemy, a view confirmed by Mussolini's organised campaign for Nice, Corsica and Tunis launched at the end of November 1938. Rearmament in the air was to be accelerated. Poland and Russia were written off as allies, the *Deuxième Bureau* duly dismissing Soviet military preparation as bluff. Against Italy, the *Comité permanente de la défense nationale*, meeting on 24 February 1939, considered various alternatives.[36] French weakness in the air which dictated the retention of French air forces in Metropolitan France inhibited serious action against Italy's African Colonies unless Britain could be persuaded to take over the air defence of northern France, as the Royal Navy had taken over the defence of France's North Sea littoral in 1912. This view, which Daladier had already put to Chamberlain in November 1938, found no echo in Britain.[37] In the staff talks held at the end of March the British reminded the French of their undertaking to protect the new BEF from the air. The French found the British obsessed by the air defence of Britain.[38]

It was the British guarantee of Poland at the end of March 1939 that really awoke the misgivings of the French High Command. Its inevitable concomitant was the approach to Russia, a revival of the whole eastern front idea, which the French army had seen disappear at Munich. The French armed forces saw no reason to alter their low opinion of the value of the Red Army and Air Force. They still worried lest the real Soviet aim was to provoke a conflict in the West.

French military plans remained the same as in 1938. The Poles were told that a French offensive of 35–38 divisions on the north-east frontier would be mounted after the fifteenth day of mobilisation.[39] They were left to infer that this would be a major offensive designed to take advantage of German military concentration against Poland. It was the general directive of 31 May,[40] which the Poles did not see, which gave the game away. The offensive promised to the Poles had become 'feeling out operations' to be undertaken in the awareness of the need to 'economise' on the use of infantry, tanks and artillery. It was only as they waited desperately for some relief from the *Blitzkrieg* of early September that the Poles realised that they had been deceived.[41]

The curiously irresponsible attitude of the French military can be seen most strongly in August 1939. The French military mission to Moscow was sent without any instructions on the crucial issue of the passage of Soviet troops through Poland and Roumania. The dispatch of Colonel Beaufre from the mission to Warsaw was not authorised in Paris.[42] The news of the Nazi–Soviet Pact which represented a total defeat for the eastern strategy was nevertheless followed by a meeting of the *Comité permanente de la défense nationale* on 23 August at which, whatever later critics might say, it is difficult not to feel that the High Command presented a more favourable view of the French position than the known facts warranted, especially in the Air Minister's remark that the air factor should not influence the government in the way it did at Munich.[43] In fact there is a good deal to be said for the theory that Gamelin was determined not to provide the defeatist French Foreign Minister, Georges Bonnet, with any arguments that would strengthen his position, and that Gamelin's own view was that France could not afford not to fight if Britain and Poland were prepared to. And yet on 2 September when the *Conseil supérieure de la guerre* met again, only two of its nineteen members, Generals Bührer and Giraud were 'resolute partisans of war'.[44] Absent in his Madrid Embassy, Marshal Pétain could speak for the remainder in denouncing the 'rash declaration of war'.[45] Nine months later the gap between Gamelin's bluff and the reality was exposed for what it was.

The underlying pessimism of the French General Staff did not prevent the French Government from following a foreign policy largely dictated by that followed by Britain. France found herself at war with Germany in September 1939 because the right wing, the future collaborators and *Vichyssoise*, could not persuade French opinion that Hitler was a better alternative to the aid provided by Britain. For them to triumph needed that defeat which was always on the cards since German rearmament began.

In the case of the German army and navy, control over strategic planning had passed irretrievably out of their hands in February 1938 with the crisis provoked by the resignation of Field Marshal von Blomberg and the trumping up of homosexual charges against the Commander-in-Chief of the Army, General Fritsch. The establishment of the OKW, swiftly followed by the occupation of Austria, created an entirely new strategic situation at a moment when Hitler had finally provided himself with the machinery for exploiting it. He began in April 1938 by considering the prospects of a *coup de main* against Czechoslovakia.[46] His military minions, Jodl and Keitel, dragged their heels a little on the plans, knowing that their implementation depended on Hitler's success in persuading Mussolini to conclude an alliance. But as the Führer's visit to Italy in early May 1938 was an unmitigated disaster, Keitel's draft of 20 May indicated that the new orders were simply a revamping of the old Case Green to cover the period until the winter of 1938–9, when new orders would have to be issued anyway.[47] At that point international nervousness led to a war scare, limited Czech mobilisation and a British and French *démarche* in Berlin. Hitler was infuriated into ordering preparations for an attack in Czechoslovakia to be timed for the end of September 1938.[48]

The course of the September crisis and the Munich conference obviated the need to put these orders into operation and left Hitler frustrated in his desire for war. The outcome of his brooding was a complicated plan to mop up Czechoslovakia, reach a permanent agreement with Poland over Danzig and the Corridor, and conclude a military alliance with Italy and Japan, adequate to distract and weaken Britain and America. The military thinking behind this was revealed in a document of 26 November 1938 designed for use in staff talks with Italy.[49] It envisaged a knock-out attack on France through the Maginot Line, with the aim of depriving Britain of her main ally on the European mainland. These orders were in turn overtaken in April when the breakdown of the German–Polish negotiations, consequent on the German occupation of Prague and the Memelland, led to the preliminary draft of orders for an attack on Poland,[50] orders which were confirmed in May after the signature of the Pact of Steel alliance with Italy and the openings of the conversations destined to lead to the Nazi–Soviet Pact.[51] The troops in fact moved up to the frontiers on 25 August only to be recalled at the last minute when it became clear that Italy was welching on her alliance, and that Britain would not seize on the Nazi–Soviet Pact as an excuse for withdrawing from her guarantee of Poland. Failing to manufacture a new way of getting Britain off the hook, Hitler went ahead with the attack on Poland on 1 September. The British ultimatum followed on 3 September—and war.

Faced with this relentless onrush into war with Britain, the members of the German General Staff failed to maintain their cohesion or to develop any feasible alternative. Their principal weakness lay in the position and character of von Brauchitsch, the new Commander-in-Chief, a man overweighed with the responsibilities of his office. But the isolation from the generality of the German nation imposed during the Seeckt regime, of which many were only too conscious, made the General Staff helpless before the increasing Nazification of the junior officers taken in after the introduction of conscription. Nor did the short-run events always confirm the soundness of their long-term judgement. Only too often they seemed to confirm the views of Hitler and his supporters. The bulk of the generals reacted by withdrawal into *Nursoldatentum*, circumscribing their activities into the purely military round of duties and business. Their opposition and doubts were well known to Hitler who, from the summer of 1939 until November 1939, gave himself repeated opportunities for confronting their arguments and opposing them with his own alternative view of the strategic realities of the day. That many of his audience were only too conscious of the revolutionary nature of the times through which they were living only weakened their assurance and confidence in their own judgement. His very success seemed to underline that he, rather than his opponents, understood aright the world around them.

Thus when one talks of the opposition within the General Staff and the officer corps to Hitler one is talking in terms of manifestations in which often only a few acknowledged leader figures were involved. They had up to a point the sympathies of the mass of their colleagues, but not their support or their certainties. Having said this, one can distinguish three phases in the opposition between February 1938 and September 1939: one of vocal opposition associated with General Beck, one of conspiracy associated with General Halder and one of despairing international intrigue which is probably best connected with Colonel Oster and Admiral Canaris of the *Abwehr*. With the outbreak of war the last two phases, conspiracy and intrigue are repeated, until the victories of 1940–42 and the defeats of 1943 reopened the issue again.

The reasoning behind the opposition can best be seen in the period of open vocal opposition, the Beck era. This opened with the Hitler–Keitel conference of 21 April 1938 already referred to and with a lengthy counter memorandum directed to von Brauchitsch by General Beck on the 'current position of Germany from the viewpoint of military policy'.[52] Beck reckoned Germany to be confronted with the hostility of Britain, France and Russia, with Britain able to call at will on American industry. In a German war on Czechoslovakia, France and Britain would certainly fight on Czechoslovakia's side. Against such a coalition Germany was simply too weak to engage in a long war. As an ally in such a war Italy would be useless. Germany therefore simply had to find a solution to the Czech problem that was acceptable to Britain.

Beck's memorandum failed to get past Brauchitsch and Keitel. Instead Hitler made the aftermath of the weekend crisis the occasion for a lengthy address to senior military officers on 28 May,[53] following this two days later with the revised draft for Case Green, beginning: 'It is my unalterable decision to smash Czechoslovakia at the first available opportunity.'[54] Beck's second memorandum of 29 May[55] accepted many of

Hitler's presuppositions but concentrated on a detailed refutation of Hitler's views on the current international situation. He went on, however, to propose a reorganisation of the procedures by which military advice was given to Hitler, one which would clearly establish a monopoly position for the Army High Command and side-track the OKW. From this he was to go on to argue that for the army leadership to proceed with Hitler's planned war would be to destroy the confidence the army and the people had in the army leadership. This brought him to his final proposal, the establishment of a collective view among the military commanders of divisions, which it would be von Brauchitsch's over-all responsibility to put to Hitler. Failing this he proposed a collective resignation—a generals' strike in fact. Behind that, in Beck's view, lay the necessity for a showdown with the SS.

Beck's proposals failed to move the senior generals at the meeting von Brauchitsch called for 4 August 1938, despite their complete acceptance of his strategic views.[56] Von Reichenau was able to warn them how violently Hitler would react to it. And General Bussch spoke for the soldierly duty of obedience and abstention from political intervention. Hitler's counter orations of 10 August on the Berghof and on 15 August on the Jütenborg training area showed how seriously he took Beck's arguments.[57] The generals seem to have remained equally unconvinced. But act they would not. Beck's resignation brought this phase to an end.

Beck's successor as Chief of Army Staff was General Halder. At this stage he shared Beck's views. Hitler's order of 17 August, removing the numerical limits previously set on SS recruiting and recognising them as standing troops in peace as well as war, brought home to many the weakened position of the army on Beck's defeat.[58] The beginning of September brought with it clear signs of the closeness of war and the accuracy of Beck's analysis. Halder turned to conspiracy, planning with General von Witzleben, Commander of Military District III, in which Berlin lay, to seize Hitler and act against the SS the moment it became clear that war with the West was inevitable. As part of the conspiracy intermediaries were dispatched to London to try to ensure that Hitler was not granted all he wanted. Here they met with incredulity and obstruction. Chamberlain compared them with the Jacobites at the court of Louis XVI, romantic has-beens dreaming of a return to the heyday of Prussian Junkerdom.[59] Their hints of a *coup*, their inability to speak plainly, and the parallels between their action and the missions of more outright Nazi fellow-travellers like Captain Wiedemann,[60] made them unwelcome if not incomprehensible. Moreover, Chamberlain's deep-rooted fear of war and feeling of personal responsibility made him the last man likely to gamble war and peace on the probability of an anti-Nazi *coup*. His sudden appearance at Berchtesgarden led the way to a solution which, while far from satisfying Hitler or deciding the issue between himself and Beck, gave the crisis an ending at the expense of the unfortunate Czech end of the balance of industrial power in central Europe, one which deprived the whole conspiracy of any *raison d'être*.

For the bulk of the German people Munich came as a deliverance. For the younger officers and generals who had believed him to be bluffing it was a triumph for Hitler. It destroyed the self-confidence, the inner security of even the core of the opposition. It drew men like Beck away from an opposition based on pragmatic arguments into one based on moral rejection of Nazism and of Hitler's leadership. Hitler made a clean sweep of three generals he knew to be disaffected. He followed this up with an instruction specifically removing the responsibility of the staff officers for the advice given and by an address at the Kroll Opera House on 10 February 1939 to a group of senior commanders.[61] Goering and von Ribbentrop copied him. The term *Militärpolitik* was forbidden as a military intervention into political matters. Von Brauchitsch made himself an echo of much of this. Despite their feelings of rage and contempt, the army stood by and did nothing while the anti-Jewish pogrom of 10–11 November 1938, the *Reichskristallennacht* raged.

Under these circumstances the best the hard core of the opposition could do was to organise their own network of contacts and explore for recruits within the closed social milieux to which their members had easy access. There were a few exploratory missions to Britain, though Colonel Schwerin was the only known military contact.[62] His mission was less to warn than to explore. The opposition's hand, or rather that of Admiral Canaris and Colonel Oster, can be seen much more clearly in the provision of untrue, alarmist but convincing reports of Hitler's plans to British intelligence sources. Four instances of these can so far be identified: the reports of a German invasion of the Netherlands probably coupled with an all-out air attack on London to take place around 21 February 1939 which reached the British via various sources in late December and early January 1939, and which gave rise to the British request to France for staff talks;[63] the information given to Mr Ian Colvin on his expulsion from Berlin at the end of March 1939, pointing to an imminent German attack on Poland which played an important part in the hasty issue of the British guarantee to Poland;[64] the warning of a planned German air attack on the Fleet which led Lord Stanhope to his somewhat over-alcoholic revelation of the warning to the British press on April 1939;[65] and the provision to the British Embassy in Berlin via Mr Louis Lochner, the American journalist, of a very much doctored version of what were probably Admiral Canaris's notes of Hitler's speech at the Berghof on

22 August 1939.[66] The aim behind all this—and very effective
it was, too—was to stir the British in 1939 to take a stronger
and more resolute position towards Hitler than they had the
previous year.

The *Abwehr*'s carefully planted pieces of misinformation
succeeded where Ewald von Kleist-Schmenzin and Colonel
Böhm-Tettelbach had failed the previous year, largely because
of the change which had come over the senior defence staffs
with the progress of the British rearmament effort. For the
Chiefs of Staff and their juniors 1936 and 1937 were the worst
years, years when nothing seemed able to prevent Britain's
inevitable defeat. Ismay, Hankey, Hollis and others have left
records of the terrible burden of anxiety that lay upon them.[67]
The worst period was almost certainly the winter of 1937–8
when, having decided that the army should not be organised
'with a military prepossession in favour of a Continental commitment',[68] to use the words of the new Secretary for War, Mr
Hore-Belisha, the Cabinet sacked the CIGS, Sir Cyril Deverell,
the Adjutant General, Sir Harry Knox, and the rest of the
Army Council.

It was at this time that the Chiefs of Staff sought to prevent
any staff talks with the French on the straightforward political
grounds that this would alienate Germany,[69] provoking
Anthony Eden to write, 'I cannot help believing that what the
Chiefs of Staff would really like to do is to re-orientate our
foreign policy and to clamber on the bandwagon with the
dictators even though that process meant parting company
with France and estranging our relations with the United
States.'[70]

The Chiefs of Staff could, perhaps, be forgiven for resenting
such a misconception, though Sir Maurice Hankey was capable
of exhibiting marked antipathy to both the French and the
Americans while at the same time expressing his admiration

for Mussolini's regime in Italy.[71] They knew that the refusal
to accept a Continental commitment was a nonsense in military
terms and that once war broke out in Europe, the curious concept of limited liability would be the first casualty. But they
were confronted with a situation in which sentiment in the
House of Commons was entirely opposed to the provision of a
Continental army and the leading professional proponent of
this opposition sat in Mr Hore-Belisha's office as his personal
adviser.

The Army Estimates enshrining the limited liability army
were introduced into the Commons on 10 March 1938. Two
days later Hitler's troops occupied Austria. The French pressed
for staff talks; the Chiefs of Staff found themselves overruled.
Their professional alarm had already been expressed in
December 1937: 'We cannot foresee the time when our defence
forces will be strong enough to safeguard our trade, territory
and vital interests against Germany, Italy and Japan at the
same time ... they could not exaggerate the importance ... of
any political or international action which could be taken to
reduce the number of our potential enemies and to gain the
support of potential allies...'[72] In March they reiterated their
view that if a prolonged struggle with Germany took place,
'... it is more than probable that both Italy and Japan would
seize the opportunity to further their own ends and that in
consequence the problem we have to envisage is not that of
limited European war only but of world war.'[73] Such a war
Britain did not have the resources to win. This remained the
view of the Chiefs of Staff throughout the summer of 1938.
Their warning was repeated to the government early in
September 1938.

The Munich Settlement delivered the immense Skoda armament works over into German hands any time they wished to
seize it. It also destroyed the thirty-five-division-strong Czech

army. Pressure on Britain to make up these deficiencies would have been expected almost immediately. Indeed, before Chamberlain's visit to Paris in November 1938, the French press were already beginning to talk in terms of *un effort du sang*. Conscription was only eight months away. In the light of everything one would expect the Chiefs of Staff to have retained the black pessimism of the summer of 1938. Such an expectation would be disappointed.

The Chiefs of Staff began, it is true, in November by opposing inter-army staff talks as tending to commit the UK to more detailed participation in French military planning than was desirable.[74] By January 1939, however, all had been changed. The instrument was the war scare of mid-January caused by the falsified reports of an imminent German attack on the Netherlands. The Chiefs of Staff admitted that British intervention would bring in Italy and possibly Japan and that this would impose a very severe strain on the Empire: 'If we were compelled to enter such a war in the near future we should be confronted with a situation more serious than the Empire has ever faced before.'[75] Nevertheless the Chiefs of Staff recommended war. In such a case 'failure to intervene would have such moral and other repercussions as would seriously undermine our position in the eyes of the Dominions and the world in general ... Failure to take up such a challenge would place Germany in a predominant position in Europe.' This change was followed by agreement on the initiation of staff talks with France, and by mid-February 1939 the Cabinet had been induced to accept the provision of a BEF of five regular and four territorial divisions with two mobile divisions at a full Continental scale of armaments.[76]

There followed in swift succession the doubling of the Territorial Army, the issues of guarantees for Poland, Roumania, Greece and Turkey and the introducton of conscription.

These measures scattered much of the regular divisions in training *cadres* for the new intakes. But although the military grumbled, their main efforts were devoted to sharpening their knives for the Secretary of State, Mr Hore-Belisha; there is little or none of the profound pessimism which is so marked a feature of the private papers of 1936–7. The tone, for example, of the Chiefs of Staff European Appreciation of 1939–40, produced in February of that year, is grim but not hopeless.[77]

This change in mood is difficult to explain in any realistic terms. Partly it is a matter of personnel, but only in part. Partly it is a consciousness of an armaments effort which was beginning to be seen to pay off—in new aircraft, in ships, in anti-aircraft guns and searchlights. In part it seems to have arisen from a conviction that Munich brought the time of illusions to an end. It echoes a remarkable change in public opinion towards Germany, a change reflected in the increasing flow of volunteers into the Territorial Army, as in the collapse of the anticipated resistance to conscription.[78] It enters also in a conviction that at last the priorities are right—that Britain's frontiers lay on the Rhine and must be defended there, all else being secondary. Finally, the sheer historical familiarity of a struggle to prevent the European Continent being dominated by a single tyranny—something Britain had never failed to prevent in the past—eliminated many of the doubts and divided counsels.

In the approach to war in 1939, among both British and Germans, one can trace the emergence of a stronger consciousness of Europe. The growing self-confidence of the British military made this express itself basically in strategic terms. The army, of course, benefited greatly from a Continental war, since only in such a war was the army's role central to Britain's war effort. Confidence in the French army was enormous so that even among those sections of the army most attuned to

France and to the ways of France, the liaison officers and the Field Security Police, one finds in their memories of the winter of 1939–40 repeated over and over again the same statement: we saw what was happening, and we did not believe.[79] What was happening was the slow collapse of French morale at all levels, encouraged by pro-Fascists on one hand, by the French Communist party on another, both extensions of the European-wide civil war of which I spoke in the first chapter. Long before the German offensive opened on 8 May 1940, France had become a major battlefield in that war. The French military leadership had nothing to put against it, neither in peace nor in war.

The opposition among the German General Staff and the bureaucracy had more. But they had become completely isolated from the mainstream of German life by their reactions to the defeat of 1918 and the Weimar experience, choosing deliberate encapsulation in their professions and the social milieux which surrounded them. The degree to which the Hitlerian challenge intentionally threatened the values which they cherished struck them only very slowly, and their opposition developed from the professional to the moral plane with equal slowness. But as it developed, so they began to look outside Germany to a wider sphere of reference. They looked, inevitably, not to France but to Britain, and they looked increasingly within a European framework: that is to say, they appealed to an idealised political and ethical system which they thought of as common to the culture of Europe. They looked to Britain for a variety of reasons. Her strength as a power, her social stability, her liberal institutions, her common Protestant faith, her monarchy, all were attractive. And in that attraction the German military found themselves up against the ultimate conflict of loyalties, of loyalty to state and loyalty to principles, culture, social conditioning, religion. For most the conflict was too great. Some it was to take into treason: Fabian von Schlabrendorff's warning to the British Embassy in August 1939 of the true conspirators;[80] Colonel Oster's warning to the Dutch of the imminence of the German attack;[81] General Beck's contact with the British Government via the Vatican. There were many others working for Britain quietly and patiently whose role is still unknown. The fate of Otto John is an indication of the degree to which, even in post-war Germany, such activities did not command any general understanding.[82]

The pity is that after Dunkirk they commanded little more in Britain. David Astor has recorded the outraged reaction of one senior British officer to Count Schwerin's visit in 1939 that it was 'damned cheek'.[83] Perhaps Hitler's position smacked too much of old-style Prussian militarism. The war revived the deep hatreds of Germany fostered by the propaganda of 1914–18, so that when the British army re-entered Germany in 1944–5, it came as a conquering force not as a liberator.

6 Experiences and Lessons of the War and its Aftermath

The years 1939–45 saw the destruction of pre-war, inter-war Europe as a socio-political organisation and as a political system. The French army, relying on a mistaken doctrine which it was itself unable to challenge without putting its position in French political society at hazard, went down in irretrievable defeat in May and June 1940. In so doing, by ruling out of court any continuation of the war from the overseas bases in southern and western Africa, it revealed its dominant Eurocentricity. And as its leaders forced the acceptance of an armistice on the government of the day, its reward was self-perpetuation in the limited form permitted by the German armistice terms, as an essential part of the system of presidential dictatorship which we call Vichy France. In November 1942, the Germans responded to the Allied invasion of North Africa by overrunning unoccupied France and disbanding the armistice army. A substantial part of the total French armistice forces had, however, been stationed in North Africa. Here, despite its initial resistance to the Anglo-American invasion forces, it was to become by far the largest part of the French army which was to accompany the Americans in the invasion of southern France and was to fight on the extreme right wing of the assault on Germany. Purges and budget cuts in the years 1944–6 were to diminish its numbers but not to destroy its fundamental nature. The army of the Fourth and Fifth Republics is still essentially the army of the

Third, with its distinguishing characteristics enhanced rather than diminished by its experience. Only its frame of reference has changed out of all recognition.

The Italian army, as we have seen, abdicated most of its serious responsibilities in 1922 when it failed to take the necessary measures to preserve the Italian state, in return for assurances that its own position and that of the monarchy would be unaffected. Mussolini attempted to play a role on the European stage well beyond the strength of his country; and although the Italian Chiefs of Staff helped preserve Italian neutrality in 1939, they, like Mussolini, were swept away by the fall of France. It was then that their neglect of their professional responsibilities both in technology and in leadership was revealed in a series of ignominious defeats, in Greece in 1940 and in the western desert. Only the long-drawn-out resistance of the Italian forces in Ethiopia under the Duke of Aosta went some way to redeem Italy's honour. In 1943, confronted with demands that Germany's southern flank should be defended to the last drop of Italian blood, army leaders backed the Crown and the Fascist Grand Council in getting rid of Mussolini and replacing him with Marshal Badoglio. The army's reward was to be torn in two: in the north and outside Italy it was ignominiously disarmed by its former ally, and only a scrappy militia permitted to the puppet Italian Republic of Saló; in the south it was treated by the British and Americans as a source of labour, a coolie-army, and its officers mocked and humiliated.

The German army abandoned its European position when its leaders failed to overthrow Hitler at the last opportunity presented to them in November 1939. Its reward was a string of victories which lasted unbroken until the winter of 1941 and the débâcle before Moscow. At that moment Hitler finally took over. The victories of 1942 were his; so were the defeats, at Stalingrad, El Alamein, and in the last offensive before Kursk in June 1943. Thereafter the German army was in retreat, caught between a supreme commander whose orders were governed by a political vision that had increasingly little to do with reality and the immense superiority in resources of the encircling enemy. The enormous technical skill of its *Nursoldaten* kept the German army in action and in being right up to the ultimate surrender; it was thus only just that Hitler's successor should be a service officer, albeit from the navy, Admiral Doenitz. Politically, however, it failed entirely. In internal matters it was unable to avoid complicity in many of the most revolting of Nazi war-crimes. Externally, even its hard core of anti-Nazis, those who organised the last desperate attempt on Hitler's life on 20 July 1944, failed to break the impression that they supported Hitler's ends and objected only to his failure. As a result the German General Staff was cited as a criminal organisation at the Nuremberg war crimes trials, and a succession of army leaders had to stand trial on war crimes charges. The armies of the post-war Germanies were to develop out of separate strands in the German military tradition. But they were to perpetuate the divided nature of post-war Germany in their own separate development.

The last of the armed forces of the major European powers were those of Britain. In accordance with long-standing tradition, they suffered a series of humiliating defeats in the initial years of war, in Norway, at Dunkirk, in Greece and Crete, in the western desert in the summer of 1942 and in the Far East where, in Singapore, British and Imperial forces surrendered to a Japanese army inferior in everything except leadership and morale.

A ruthless political leadership found alternative commanders within its ranks and its material requirements were made up from the endless resources of the United States. But the effect of the defeats was to increase Britain's sense of isolation from Europe and to drive its élites, including the military, to seek alternative frames of reference, alternative systems, in the concepts of an overseas Commonwealth or an Atlantic community, with a super-power with a Pacific and an Arctic coast-line. Internally the eviction of British forces from Europe once more destroyed the balance between the three branches of the armed forces. Thus, in 1945 the whole issue of an imperial versus a continental versus an apocalyptic deterrent strategy, which had so bedevilled strategic planning before 1938, was reopened. And, as in the inter-war years, the inexorable pressure of economics and geography was needed to resolve the debate twenty years later.

These then must be the themes of this last chapter. To begin with France: the German break-through at Sedan and its brilliant exploitation struck the French Cabinet of M. Reynaud with panic. Tied hand and foot as French parliamentarians of the Third Republic were to historical tradition, M. Reynaud turned to those representatives of French military history, Marshal Pétain and General Weygand, the surrogate Foch. Hopes were pinned on a new miracle of the Marne. Weygand took only two steps, both of them significant. On 21 May he ordered an offensive into the corridor to Abbeville held by the Germans separating the armies of Flanders from those of France.[1] Faulty liaison produced little more than a brief British foray around Arras. The second was his order of 26 May 1940 that the line on the Somme was to be held '*sans esprit de recul*', an order which meant inevitably that if that line was broken, an armistice was to be preferred to a retreat to North Africa or a Breton redoubt.[2] The civilian members of the *Comité de Guerre*, meeting on 25 May to endorse Weygand's order failed to understand its military implications, pinning their hopes on an American declaration of war or a full committal of British *air* forces to battle, when unused modern fighter aircraft and tanks, to a number in excess of those demanded of Britain, lay scattered the length and breadth of France.[3]

Confronted with defeat and the military demand that an armistice be sued for, the Reynaud Cabinet was lost. Weygand's refusal to resign or to execute any orders other than those they desired, his insistence that the Reynaud Cabinet in no way represented France, left Reynaud no alternative. Having preferred age and prestige to youth and a new vision, the civilians, in essence, abdicated. The regime of Marshal Pétain was the regime of the army leadership. All but a handful of maverick officers abided by their professional loyalties even in defeat. And after the British attack on the French fleet at Oran and the failure of the Free French expedition to Dakar, the military even toyed with the idea of a *renversement des alliances*.[4] The principal Free French leaders, General de Gaulle, General Catroux, General le Gentilhomme, Colonel de Larminat, Admiral Muselier, were tried *in absentia* and sentenced to death and deprivation of citizenship.[5]

The French army was to be reduced to 120,000 officers and men under the terms of the armistice. The effect was to make possible a retrenchment on a very narrow social base. The eight thousand officers allowed to continue in service were drawn largely from the *grandes écoles*. Jews, Freemasons, the promoted rankers and reservists of the First World War were all removed. In 1946 graduates of St Cyr formed a much higher proportion of the higher officer corps than in 1938.[6]

The circumstances of the Vichy regime obviated any examination of the causes of the defeat of 1940 in terms of French military doctrine, material or tactics. The lessons of 1940 were seen in terms of morale. The leaders of the armistice army sought to preach the need for a new army fired by enthusiasm, passion, faith.[7] Its training programmes emphasised physical fitness, military punctilio, parade ground smartness, privation, discipline. Athletics, even the encouragement of dare-devil stunts, played a part inconceivable in the army of garrisoned conscripts of the inter-war years. Cavalry returned to the horse —or the bicycle. Behind this lay the idea of the slow recovery of French national greatness by the creation of a new spirit in the military élite which was seen as the essential guarantor of social order, the cement that bound the nation together. France had been betrayed by her allies. In future France must rely on herself, *la France seule*. Anglophobia was fanned by such episodes as Dakar and the British occupation of Syria in 1941 and Madagascar in 1942. Germanophobia fed on the German refusal to repatriate the million and a half French prisoners of war or to allow recruiting for the armistice army in occupied France.

The events of November 1942 revealed much of this to be based on illusion. Only in Tunisia did French forces resist the German takeover, and then too late. De Lattre de Tassigny, attempting to organise resistance in France, was arrested and sentenced to ten years.[8] His escape gave France her ablest war-time commander. Hitler dissolved the French metropolitan army. Laval saved one honorary regiment, the First French Regiment. Some regulars went into the underground and raised units bearing names of famous French regiments. But their role was limited by their unwillingness to accept a war of sabotage and assassination. Before June 1944 the time was not ripe for the emergence of a large-scale *maquis* as was shown by the fate of the Ghéres *maquis* and the Vercors in the Dauphiné. The *Organisation de Résistance de l'Armée* was very effective in stopping German military movements from south-west France towards Normandy in July 1944: but the main role in the *maquis* was taken by the left.[8]

The 120,000-strong French army in North Africa was another matter. They fought strongly against the allied landing parties in Algiers and Oran until a formula was found in the person of the infamous Darlan to allow for a transfer of loyalties. They were then to form the main part of the First French Army which invaded southern France under de Lattre de Tassigny. The Gaullist divisions of Leclerc and Koenig, despite their valiant record at Bir Hacheim, were, with only 15,000 men, simply swallowed up in the new army. General de Gaulle's determination to unite rather than divide France made him behave towards them with almost Bourbon ingratitude.

The officer corps in France at the time of liberation was not so fortunate. The *maquis* and *épuration* led to 12,000 of the pre-war officer corps being pensioned off, 658 being dismissed without pension.[9] Armistice army commanders, except for those few who had redeemed themselves by *maquis* work or escape to North Africa were tried. But the army was able to outstay the *maquis*. Although 137,000 were incorporated from the French forces of the Interior into de Lattre de Tassigny's armies, few attained any rank above the most junior. Further dismissals of officers in the 1946 budget's *dégagement des cadres*, a substantial reduction of the post-war forces, paradoxically increased the hold of the long-term army officer corps. A quiet revenge was taken on the Gaullist officers who had 'broken discipline' by joining de Gaulle before November 1942. Instead, men such as Charles Ailleret or Paul Ely, three times Chief of Army Staff, whose ranks in the armistice army had been confirmed by the 1944-6 army as a recognition of their service in the underground, saw their way to the top.[10]

The lot of the Italian army, as noted earlier, was much harder, and little attention has yet been paid to it by the military historian. In 1940 the Italian General Staff had hugged to itself the illusion that in entering the war against France it was embarking, not on a disreputable trip among the *Wehr-macht*'s camp followers, but on a parallel war, waged in accordance with what they conceived to be Italian aims and desires.[11] Their experience at the hands of the German armistice commissioners should have convinced them that this was a misconception. But it was a misconception which was created by their own inability to deliver any victories to match those of their German ally. To do the army chiefs justice, they had done their level best in the spring of 1940 to warn Mussolini of the deplorable state of Italy's army. It was without modern artillery, without tanks, without tracked cross-country transport. Only a few divisions were above two-thirds strength, and it depended on the import of raw material from abroad whose loss it was far from clear that Germany either could or would make up. But the illusion that Italy could stage a war limited to eleven divisions, of which only seven could actually take part in the operations against a Greek enemy whose full armed forces amounted to three times that figure, and whose divisions were one-third as strong again as their own,[12] was the contribution of the Italian General Staff alone. The Greek victories in Epirus were followed by those of Wavell in the western desert, the victory of a small modern mobile army with tanks against an army of parades and road-bound vehicles. In each case German intervention was necessary to prevent an irretrievable Italian defeat.

The Italian experience as Germany's ally was an unhappy one. Italy's units always came second to the *Afrika Korps* for supplies and mobility, and at El Alamein they were abandoned, after putting up a stout defence against the Eighth Army.[13] In Tunisia the Germans surrendered where some Italians wished to continue fighting.[14] And in Sicily, once the allied landings had been successful, it became clear to the Italian General Staff that Italy was being sacrificed to delay a direct attack on Germany, or as the OKW war diary put it, to keep the war as far as possible away 'from the heart of Europe and thus from the German frontier'.[15] Hitler's total preoccupation with the Kursk offensive at the time was not lost on them—nor was the ease with which German reinforcements became available once Mussolini's fall had confronted Hitler with the threat of Italy's withdrawal from the war.[16]

Nevertheless the substitution of a Badoglio Government for that of Mussolini appears to have been the work of the King and a dissident group in the Fascist Grand Council rather than of the Army High Command. They made an armistice in despair, amidst signs of an imminent German take-over. But they made it also under the illusion that their navy and army would be welcome allies to the Anglo–American forces. It was an illusion soon to be dispelled. The Italian declaration of war and co-belligerency did not spare them an occupation policy quite as harsh in its own way, if not more so, than that the Germans imposed on northern Italy, resurrected into the puppet state of Saló. Saló was even allowed its own army, of unwilling conscripts and desperate volunteers, trusted by the Germans to hold the Maritime Alps against invasion from France and melting away by the thousand after the allied invasion of southern France in September 1944.[17] Only the commanders of Saló were to face trial after 1945. Otherwise, like the French, the Italian army was to continue the same as before.

By 1938, Hitler had already brought about a social revolution in Germany which had deprived the German army leadership and officer corps of its old position in the state. This social revolution did not lie, as Nazi propagandists often claimed it did, in the creation of a state where all the racially pure were equal, *Volksgenossen* one and all. Wealth and social prestige continued as the rewards of success. Military-style ranks and hierarchies were multiplied to feed the vanity of the lower-middle-class *arrivistes* who made up so large a part of the Nazi leadership. Hitler destroyed the survivals of the imperial *Ständesstadt*, the state based on separate orders, and he destroyed, above all, the dominant position the army occupied as the *Stand*, the order, whose co-signature was essential to the business of the state.[18] When the army leadership failed to support General Beck's doctrine of military co-responsibility, and when they accepted the commission of the SS as *Waffenträger*, professional corporate bearers of arms, they surrendered the separate position of strength from which the army had hitherto operated and stumbled unknowingly into that of a beleaguered minority.[19]

It was Germany's peculiar sorrow that the ideals of that minority were in general more civilised than and much more preferable to the ideals and morals of those who supplanted them, and that joining the majority meant adopting the concern for the defeated of the SS and the respect for human dignity of the SD. The alternative was a military dictatorship, a *coup d'état* or *pronunciemento* on Latin American lines, in which an essential was the immediate arrest, if not the assassination of the man to whom their personal oath of loyalty had been given. More than that, a *coup* would have to be followed by an armistice and a settlement which, to be acceptable to Hitler's external enemies, would entail the abandonment of German hegemony in Europe and the charge of treason not merely against the state but against the nation, not merely *Staatsverrat* but *Landesverrat*.

The junior generals whom von Seeckt had trained were singularly unsuited for so bold and blind a stride into politics. In the end the plans for a *coup* in November 1939 failed for the lack of a commander to give the order to proceed.[20] Central to that failure was the havering indecision of General von Brauchitsch. Without his order no other unit would proceed;

and while his indecision increased and multiplied from day to day under the pressure of Hitler's brutal attacks on the spirit of Zossen (where the General Staff had its headquarters), the courage and determination of the army command melted away and the shame and dishonour of the SS excesses during the Polish campaign, which had once determined so many on action, became more and more easy to forget. For long the army leadership had reconciled itself to the domestic excesses of Nazism by considering them as the unavoidable concomitants of national renewal or as the excesses of individuals rather than as the indispensable core of the Nazi system itself.

It is worth emphasising this lack of a central command in the German officer corps and the failure of the individuals in command in 1938-9 to rise to their individual responsibilities; since, by contrast with this, the emergence of the military conspirators in 1942-3 from among the younger members of the staff corps takes on the character of a collective decision of a minority, even a small minority, arising from their sense of alienation from and disgust with the Germany created by Hitler. Not for them the illusions of their elders, that it was not Hitler but his entourage who were to blame. The decision that he must be assassinated began as a series of individual decisions, thwarted by the accident of fate or by that sixth sense which had served Hitler before. Time ran out on the conspirators, and what in 1943 might have still been generally acceptable as the beginning of a genuine change in Germany seemed, after D-Day, to be too much like a *sauve qui peut* on the part of those whom Allied public opinion was still half convinced were the real wire-pullers behind the Nazi leadership. Churchill himself had come to see Nazism as an outgrowth of Prussian militarism, not an entirely unperceptive point of view but one which omitted any observation of the changes through which that Prussian military spirit might have passed in revulsion from the fruit it had produced.[21] Between Nazism and the values and morals of the Imperial Army Officer Corps, lay a wide gulf and genuine Prussians among Hitler's Nazi élites were a handful of social renegades only.

The tentative approaches of intermediaries from the genuine opposition were thus never distinguished from the host of other soundings which accompanied them, from the ambitious SS to the exiled politicians, the dissident military, the would-be *Abwehr* double agents, and the repentant fellow-travellers. After Schellenberg's successful impersonation of a dissident general had enabled him as a result of the Venlo incident in November 1939, to cripple the Netherlands offices of Military Intelligence and the Secret Intelligence Service together,[22] British intermediaries could be forgiven for dismissing any German initiative either as the work of an *agent provocateur* or just another rat trying to work his passage.

The Soviet Union was not so stupid. Its more than flirtation with the idea of a free German movement, its establishment in 1943 of the League of German Officers among the generals and others taken at Stalingrad hid a serious determination to see established after the war in Germany a government under Soviet influence and control.[23] The seesaw-like changes of Soviet German policy which settled in the end on infiltration by Moscow-trained Communist teams[24] rather than an appeal to the spirit of Rapallo probably represented a fairly shrewd judgement of the use that could be made of French anti-German feelings to thwart any Anglo–American insistence on the post-war economic recovery of Germany, following as it did General de Gaulle's visit to Moscow in the winter of 1944.[25] What is interesting here is the degree of response the idea of a new Rapallo evoked. To the end the conspirators of July 1944 could not decide between Russia and the West, the former Ambassador to Moscow, Werner von Schulenberg, being held in readiness as Foreign Minister to a post-Hitlerian government should the Russian approach seem more advisable.

It is doubtful, however, whether many of the younger officers, save only the would-be assassin, von Stauffenberg himself, were attracted by the idea of a new Rapallo or a revival of National Bolshevism. Their dominant ethos appears to have been of a Christian conservative kind, looking to some kind of European federation and a settlement with Britain and France rather than with Russia.[26] The excesses of Nazism and those of Bolshevism were to them indistinguishable, both threats to substitute terror for law as the basis of the state. Whatever their aims, Hitler was saved and those who did not escape into suicide or succeed in concealing their tracks were hauled one by one before Roland Freisler's courts to perish, mostly before Hitler finally took his life.

The army which surrendered in so piecemeal a fashion in May 1945 was commanded either by Nazi sycophants or by the surviving *Nursoldaten*. Many of them, like von Runstedt, Guderian, or Heinrici, had been dismissed by Hitler in the last days on specifically military issues. Too many were tarred with the stigma of complicity in the massacre of partisans or hostages, in the execution of Allied commandos or prisoners of war, for service in the German army at any but the lowest ranks to be a mark of honour or distinction.

With the surrender came the trials. At Nuremberg at the main trial the Prosecution sought unsuccessfully for a declaration that the General Staff and Supreme Command were criminal organisations. Their failure had more than a little to do with the terms of the indictment. But the Tribunal ruled that against individuals war crimes charges could be proceeded with. Their judgement of 'this collection of military officers' contained the following two paragraphs:

They have been responsible in large measure for the miseries and suffering which have fallen on millions of men, women and children. They have been a disgrace to the honourable profession of arms. Without their military guidance the aggressive ambitions of Hitler and his fellow Nazis would have been academic and sterile. Although they were not a group falling within the words of the Charter they were certainly a ruthless military caste. The contemporary German militarism flourished briefly with its recent ally, National Socialism, as well as or better than it had in the generations of the past.

Many of these men have made a mockery of the soldier's oath of obedience to military orders. When it suits their defence they say they had to obey: when confronted with Hitler's great crimes which are shown to have been within their general knowledge, they say they disobeyed. The truth is that they actively participated in all these crimes, or sat silent and acquiescent, witnessing the commission of crimes on a scale larger and more shocking than the world has ever had the misfortune to know . . .[27]

Those words, though confined by the Tribunal to the one hundred and thirty or so individuals who had held supreme command, or the position of Deputy Commander or of Chief of Staff in the three armed forces, in effect put the whole German officer corps out of European civilisation. The verdict followed naturally from the evidence of complicity in war crimes and from the definition of crimes of war agreed by the major powers of the United Nations who had set up the Tribunal. If Hitler's assault on the European system had represented, as it was clear it did, an attempt to substitute an alternative morality for that hitherto accepted, then the failure of the officer corps to prevent this involved complicity. The leading figures of the opposition had seen this in 1939.

Only the British armed forces finished on the winning side. They were to find that the victory had solved none of the dilemmas and troubles which had bedevilled British policy during the pre-war years. Victory had, it was true, produced an abler High Command in each of the three services. It had not, however, settled the question of inter-service priorities. Churchill's own very idiosyncratic methods of civilian direction of the war did not lend themselves to formal incorporation into normal governmental practice. And Britain's military commitments in Palestine, Egypt, Malaya, Greece, as well as in the occupation of Venezia, south-eastern Austria and north-western Germany seemed to commit her to a Continental and an imperial strategy at one and the same time. The grant of independence to India and Pakistan deprived her of her second army, as well as a major defence commitment. The hopes of development in Africa and the dependence on sterling—that is, Middle Eastern rather than dollar oil—made the continued exclusion of other major powers from the Middle East of continuing importance. Lastly, the use of nuclear weapons in the Far East and the refusal of Congress to honour the Churchill–Roosevelt agreements on the sharing of nuclear secrets raised again the RAF's vision of strategic deterrence, despite the comparative balance and common sense of the Air Force command at the end of the war.[28]

Britain was, in addition, caught between the dilemma of the large or the small war. The presence of very sizeable Soviet military contingents in Central Europe raised the spectre of a new large-scale war and much of the debate—the navy's six aircraft carrier programme, the RAF's desire for new long-range bombers, the army's reluctance to accept a hasty demobilisation—related to the threat that one day the mass of Russian divisions would simply get up and march westwards until the Channel stopped them. In 1946 this seemed still sufficiently remote for Field-Marshal Montgomery to assume a fifteen-year lapse of time before the armed forces need again be ready for a major war. Two years later the Czechoslovak *coup* and the blockade of Berlin made the government extend the term of conscript service by three months.

There followed a furious debate over the commitment of major land forces to a Continental campaign in which, despite the Treaty of Dunkirk and the Brussels Treaty of West European Union, the Chief of Air Staff was still arguing against any long-term commitment to the Continent save in terms of a small élite army, armoured, motorised and highly mobile, a gold medal 'limited liability' army of the 1950s.

At the same time financial crises were hitting the armed services on a scale reminiscent of the 1931–3 years. Army strength was slashed, as was that of the R A F; and while long-term development continued, short-term development was ruled out and the armed forces made to live on the residue of wartime weapons and development. As a result the armed forces found themselves in a state of schizophrenia. For twenty years they planned and prepared and thought about and held manoeuvres and war games based on a major European war against the Soviet Union. For the same twenty years their troops fought and guarded, intervened and policed in an endless series of small wars, raids, police actions and so on, most of which demanded a very high degree of mobility for very small forces. Suez, with its long and arthritic preparation for an amphibious attack, showed the perils of such a strategy when its needs were scaled up to anything above a battalion or at most a brigade. It took another two or three years before Admiral Sir Caspar John was able to use his tact and persistence as Chief of Naval Staff to obtain inter-service agreement on a combined strategy. Only two years later the cancellation of Skybolt and the imposition of Polaris on an unwilling navy destroyed most of his work in the name of a national deterrent in whose credibility few could be found to believe. Economic pressures to reduce Britain's overseas commitments finally forced the abandonment in 1967 of all but the most token of defence postures east of Suez.[29] Britain had finally been reduced to the Continental commitment she had accepted as a permanent responsibility in 1954 as the only way of securing French agreement to the rearmament of West Germany.

The most interesting element in these twenty years from the point of view of the theme of this book is the gradual acceptance by the army staff of a playing down of the European responsibilities in which Viscount Montgomery had realised their vital interest in 1946.[30] The increasing use of army units in small wars brought a return of army thinking and interest to the small wars of the nineteenth century and the need for amphibious exercises, especially after the Suez fiasco. The successful British back-up in Libya, Jordan, Aden and the Gulf of the American intervention in the Lebanon in 1958 showed how quickly the lessons had been learnt. The outstanding example however is the army's willing, indeed long-worked for, abandonment of conscription in 1958 in return for a long-term volunteer army with the merest shadow of a general reserve for overseas service. It was the cuts in the reserve that agitated the army, and the figure of voluntary recruitment fixed by Ministry of Defence statisticians. The disappearance of the immediately mobilisable, short-term reserve by which Montgomery had set so much store hardly seems to have worried them at all.

In this adjustment it can be argued the armed forces were only reflecting a neglect of a Europe safely ensconced behind the American nuclear shield which was common to all political parties and had been since the Labour Party's rejection of the Schumann and Pleven Plans had been confirmed by the Eden Government's lack of interest in the Treaty of Rome. A generation reared in the comfortable yet, as events proved, entirely bogus isolationism of the Commonwealth of Nations of the years 1920–38, was now in power, a generation that had forgotten in its bones the lessons of Locarno and Munich—that Britain must, for reasons of strategy, always respond first to movements in the balance of power in Europe, and cannot afford a Europe dominated by another power even where that power is nominally friendly. But the long debate over Europe was to reveal many other illusions in Britain.

The first of these was the degree to which the doctrines of the Vichy army, of *La France seule*, were shared by de Gaulle and embodied in the foreign policy of the Fifth Republic. The army of the Fourth Republic had, as was shown above, been formed mainly from the personnel of the armistice army. Their ideas of a France reborn morally and spiritually to regain its position of dominance in Europe after suffering and the acquisition of discipline were pure Gaullism. It was de Gaulle who was right in 1940 in picking the victor and refusing surrender, not they—and this correctness of judgement was never forgiven him. But the army of the Fourth Republic was trained and exercised along lines utterly familiar to de Gaulle's own followers by the same Colonel Schlesser as commander of St Cyr in 1946 whom we have seen leading the retraining of the second division in 1942.[31] The subsequent history of the army, isolated from the nation in two long and bitterly fought wars, both ended by political capitulation in Indo-China and in Algeria, did nothing to change matters.[32] The attempt to overthrow General de Gaulle and avert an Algerian withdrawal was an attempt to save the honour of the army of the Fourth Republic in colonial wars alone. For those who had escaped the colonial débâcles de Gaulle promised an end to a system of alliances. In NATO, whose command structure SHAPE functioned on French territory, France seemed more and more to be among the also ran. The French army had fought the European Defence Community tooth and nail, the more because of its support by the United States. General de Gaulle's expulsion of NATO and withdrawal from the military entanglements and the defence policy of arming France's missiles *à toutes azimuths* represented the epitomisation of the Vichy doctrine of *La France seule*. Only de Gaulle's France had conquered, a desperate Dr Adenauer having tied West Germany to his coat-tails by the Treaty of January 1963.

The second great illusion nurtured in Britain until at least the early 1960s was that West Germany, the Federal German Republic, set up in 1949 and permitted to rearm within the structure of NATO in 1955 by the Treaty of Paris, was the direct inheritor of the military tradition and outlook of the *Reichsheer* and *Reichswehr*. This was to ignore the circumstances and discontinuity of the German armed forces entirely. The West German Federal armed forces had their origin in the construction of two entirely separate lines of development. The first was the conviction which overtook the NATO military planners from the outset that a defence of Western Europe against attack by conventional forces was impossible without a substantial German Contribution. The second was the reaction of the Federal German Government to the creation of armed *Bereitschaften*, standing security forces, so called, in the Soviet-occupied zone.[33]

The outbreak of the Korean War provided the catalyst. Adenauer drew his advisers from the survivors of the military opposition. Count Schwerin, Adenauer's first military adviser chose his own circle (to meet in October 1950 in the Himmerod monastery) from the survivors of the opposition— General Speidel, General Heusinger, General Baron von Vietinghoff-Scheel and Colonel Count von Kielmannsegg. On Schwerin's resignation, Adenauer appointed a Catholic trades unionist, Theodor Blank in his place. Others in the original group were Wolf, Count Baudissin, and one of the unsuccessful would-be assassins of Hitler, vintage 1943, Axel Freiherr von der Bussche. These men had had five years to reflect on what had gone wrong with the *Reichswehr*. Their conclusions led directly to the three distinguishing marks of the *Bundeswehr*: its subordination to the law, the circumscription of the rights of the individual soldier and the provision of a parliamentary commissioner to report on them, and the emphasis on moral leadership, *innere Führung*.[34] This emphasis turned out to provide an excellent illustration of the theories of the functionalists, since the new *Bundeswehr* drew very heavily for its *cadres* of officers, and still more of NCOs, on the ranks of the former *Reichswehr*. The effect has been to produce an army bedevilled by problems of adjustment to a non-military society, with military trades unions to complicate matters still further. But a political army the present *Bundeswehr* most certainly is not—its influence on West German politics has been virtually nil.

For the British onlooker all this was very hard to swallow. To allow ex-Nazi generals to parade in command of troops seemed sheer lunacy—and the occasional revelation of the murky past of some German representative at NATO was a godsend to the Soviet and East German propagandists and to all those for whom a Soviet source was not an immediate reason for rejecting allegations. Indeed I myself must admit to a momentary panic when I was visiting the British Army College of the Rhine in 1959. It shared a barracks with a German unit, and I woke to see out of the window the familiar peaked caps and grey-green uniforms of the cinema's German armies; I wondered if, for a brief moment, I had been shifted to a parallel universe where the Germans had won.

This, however, was nothing to the shock of seeing the guards outside the East German War Ministry in Berlin goose-stepping as they paced their beats. The East German Army, despite its proletarian nature, originated in the technical advice of a group of former *Reichswehr* officers.[35] The first units were raised as barrack garrison police and provided with arms and armour for use in a para-military role to seize power in the event of a unified Germany coming into existence. The first commander of the East German Army, Vincenz Müller, one-time member of von Schleicher's staff and associate of General von Witzleben in his private conspiracy against Hitler in the summer of 1939, who went over to the Soviet's National Committee for a Free Germany after his capture by Soviet forces. Müller, like his opposite numbers in the Blank office, knew the importance of tradition in military life, Communist loyalty being guaranteed as in the early days of the Red Army by a structure of commissars existing parallel with the command structure at all levels.

To recapitulate briefly the theme of this book. It has been argued that in certain important respects the Second World War, particularly in the years 1939–41, was a European civil war marking the breakdown of a complicated political economic and social system, which was also a security system, erected hastily and rather uncertainly in 1919 and incorporating within itself various, often indigestible, features, survivals from the more coherent and consistent system existing before 1914. To function properly the system required the armed forces of the major powers to play a double role, within the domestic politics of their own country and externally in relation to the other powers of Europe. Internally, their role was to guarantee stability and to advise on matters of military security. Externally, their job was to observe and warn on any change in the relative balance of power and to adapt their military thinking to changes in the technology of war. For various historic reasons the armed forces of all four powers to varying degrees failed in their task, the nearest to success being the British. All to some extent failed in relation to the changing technology of war, the lead being shared equally between Germany and Britain. The reasons for these failures have been found in the historical and political relationships between the High Commands of the various branches of each nation's armed forces and the political leadership, in the powers of the military to force or persuade the politicians, and among the latter a willingness to listen and choose. Knowledge of their relative weaknesses led the military advisers of the powers to warn very strongly against war in 1938 and after, in contrast with the position in 1913–14. But their prophecies, which in nearly every case were borne out by events, were unable to withstand the clash of ideologies between radical militant integral nationalism and the ideology of method held to by the democracies. Political miscalculation based on misinformation took the civilians into war. The second collapse of Europe followed inevitably. When a new Europe emerged it was to find a world divided, a confrontation between the super-powers. It is to meet that challenge that the surviving parts of Europe came together and are now, through their historians, engaged in exploring once more a diverse past to find what they have in common to face an uncertain future.

Chapter Notes
Select Bibliography
Index

Chapter Notes

Chapter 1

1 Raymond Aron, *Paix et Guerre entre les Nations*, Paris 1962, pp. 113 ff.

2 F. S. L. Lyons, *Internationalism in Europe 1815–1914*, Leyden 1963.

3 Nils Orvik, *The Decline of Neutrality 1914–1945*, 2nd edn, London 1971.

4 Marlbone W. Graham Junior, 'The Soviet Security System', *International Conciliation*, 1929.

5 Walter H. Kaufmann, *Monarchism in the Weimar Republic*, New York 1953.

6 André Malraux, *L'Espoir*, Paris 1937. Malraux was only seventeen when the 1918 armistice was signed.

7 On the *Freikorps* movement see R. G. L. Waite, *Vanguard of Nazism*, Cambridge, Mass. 1952; Hagen Schutze, *Freikorps und Republik, 1918-1920*, Boppard am Rhein 1969. The most powerful evocation of this generation in literature is in the work of Ernst von Salomon; cf especially *die Geächteten*, Berlin 1931, *die Kadetten*, Berlin 1933, and *der Fragebogen*, Hamburg 1951.

8 For the memoirs of a British parallel with Malraux and von Salomon, see Douglas V. Duff, who served both in the Black and Tans and in the Palestine Police, *Bailing with a Teaspoon*, London 1958. Readers of Evelyn Waugh's diaries will have noted that he, too, was of this generation.

9 On which see the memoirs of Fred Copeman, *Reason in Revolt*, London 1958, who subsequently joined and left the Communist movement and was feted in Moscow.

Chapter 2

1 Arthur Rosenberg, *The Birth of the German Republic*, London 1931; Hans W. Gatzke, *Germany's Drive to the West*, Baltimore 1950; Gerhard Ritter, *The Sword and the Sceptre*, vols III and IV London 1973.

2 Jere Clemens King, *Generals and Politicians*, Berkeley, Cal. 1951.

3 See Jere Clemens King, *Foch versus Clemenceau*, Cambridge, Mass. 1960.

4 The books mentioned here are Wilfred Owen, *Poems*, London 1920; Edward Blunden, *Undertones of War*, London 1928; Edward Thomas, *Collected Poems*, London 1920; Siegfried Sassoon, *Memoirs of a Fox-Hunting Man*, London 1928 and *Memoirs of an Infantry Officer*, London 1930; Ernst von Salomon, *Die Geächteten*, Berlin 1931; C. S. Forester, *The General*, London 1936; Erich Maria Remarque, *Im Westen nichts neues*, London 1930; and Henri Barbusse, *Le Feu, Journal d'une Escouade*, Paris 1916.

5 PRO, CP 311(23).

6 United States National Archives, State Department Decimal File, 500.A 1503 Shearer, Wm. B.21, John Wilson to Castle, 26 September 1929.

7 Cited in Carlo del Biase, *L'Aquile d'Oro*, Milan 1969, p. 353.

8 Admirably examined in Richard D. Challener, *The French Theory of the Nation in Arms*, New York 1955.

9 Paul Marie de la Gorce, *The French Army*, trans. K. Douglas, London 1963, p. 184.

10 Cited in de la Gorce, p. 182.

11 de la Gorce, p. 186.

12 Cited in de la Gorce, p. 191.

13 Report of 28 May 1932 cited in Maxime Weygand, *Mémoires*, vol. II, p. 385; P. C. F. Bankwitz, *Maxime Weygand and Civil-Military Relations in Modern France*, Cambridge, Mass., 1961, p. 85.

14 Bankwitz, pp. 92, 96, 98–9.

15 Rosenberg, pp. 114, 152; Gerhard Ritter, *The Sword and the Sceptre*, vol. III, part 3 *passim*.

16 Ritter, vol. IV, p. 385; Klaus Jürgen Müller, *Das Heer und Hitler*, Stuttgart 1969, p. 14.

17 Ritter, vol. IV, p. 385.
18 Wilhelm Groener, *Lebenserinnerungen*, Göttingen 1957, p. 640; Müller, pp. 15–16.
19 Groener, p. 467.
20 Cited in Müller, p. 18, f.20.
21 These statistics are taken from Karl Demeter, *The German Officer-Corps in Society and State, 1650–1945*, trans. A. Malcolm, London 1965, p. 47.
22 Demeter, p. 54.
23 Gerhard F. Kramer, 'The Influence of National Socialism on the Courts of Justice and the Police' in *The Third Reich*, UNESCO, London 1955.
24 Golo Mann, 'Staat und Heer', in *Geschichte und Geschichten*, Frankfurt 1961; cited in Müller, p. 20, f.30.
25 See John P. Fox, 'The Formulation of Germany's Far Eastern Policy, 1933–1936', London PhD thesis, 1972.
26 On the Italian army in the years 1918–22, see Giorgio Rochat, *L'Esercito Italiano da Vittorio Veneto a Mussolini (1919–1925)*, Bari 1968; del Biase, pp. 353–69.
27 del Biase, pp. 353–4.
28 Francesco Nitti, *Rivelazioni. Dramatis Personae*, Naples 1948, p. 395.
29 del Biase, p. 360.
30 del Biase, p. 364. Adrian Lyttelton, *The Seizure of Power: Fascism in Italy, 1919–1929*, London 1973, pp. 91–2.
31 Demeter, pp. 191–2.
32 F. L. Carsten, *The Reichswehr and Politics, 1918–1933*, Oxford 1966; Thilo Vogelsang, *Reichswehr, Staat und NSDAP*, Stuttgart 1962; Sir John W. Wheeler-Bennett, *The Nemesis of Power*, London 1953; Gordon A. Craig, *The Politics of the Prussian Army 1640–1945*, Oxford 1955.
33 See Franklyn Johnson, *Defence by Committee*, London 1960.
34 Captain Stephen Roskill, RN, *Hankey, Man of Secrets*, London 1970–72.
35 Karl Dietrich Bracher, Wolfgang Sauer, Gerhard Schulz, *Die Nationalsozialistische Machtergreifung*, Köln 1960, p. 729, citing the evidence of General, later Ambassador, Eugen Ott of General von Reichenau's directive to commanding officers of February 1933.
36 Müller, pp. 61–87.
37 Karl-Othmar Frhr. von Aretin, 'Der Eid auf Hitler', *Politische Studien*, 7, 1957; Müller, pp. 134–9.

38 Wolfgang Foerster, *Generaloberst Ludwig Beck*, Munich 1960, p. 60; Müller, pp. 206 ff.

39 *Nuremberg Documents*, 139-C.

40 Beck to Fritsch, 3 May 1935, cited by Müller, p. 211.

41 *Nuremberg Documents*, Keitel-9; Müller, p. 241.

42 Müller, pp. 216–32.

43 *Nuremberg Documents*, C-175.

44 *Documents on German Foreign Policy*, Series D, vol. I, No. 19; Müller, p. 243.

45 Beck to Fritsch, 20 May 1937; Forster, p. 62; Müller, pp. 235–7.

46 del Biase, pp. 378–88. Giorgio Rochat, 'Mussolini et les forces armées' in *La Guerre en Méditerranée, 1939–45* (Actes du Colloque Internationale), Paris 1971.

47 del Biase, pp. 379, 393–5, citing Alessandro Lessona, *Memorie. Al governo con Mussolini*, Roma 1968, pp. 165 ff. See also Giorgio Rochat, *Militari e Politici nella Preparazione della Campagna d'Etiopia*, Milan 1971.

48 del Biase, pp. 416–20; Rochat, 'Mussolini...', pp. 53–6.

49 *Foreign and Commonwealth Office Library*, German Naval Archives, Photostats, M70/M002233, M002219–20, M002229.

50 Enno von Rintelen, *Mussolini als Bundesgenosse*, Tubingen 1951.

51 See *D.G.F.P.*, Series D, vol. VI, Appendix I; *I Documenti Diplomatici Italiani*, Ottava Serie, vol. XIII, Appendici III e IV; Mario Toscano, 'Le Conversazioni militari italo-tedesche alla vigilia della seconda guerra mondiale,' *Rivista storica italiana*, LXIV, 1952.

52 Bankwitz, pp. 36–40.

53 Bankwitz, pp. 76–82.

54 Bankwitz, pp. 103–4, summarizes the minutes of the meeting.

55 Thomas Emmerson, 'The Reoccupation of the Rhineland. A Study in Multilateral Diplomacy', London PhD Thesis, 1973.

56 Lieutenant Colonel Jean Vial, 'La défense nationale; son organisation entre les deux guerres', *Revue d'Histoire de la deuxième guerre mondiale*, 18, 1953.

57 PRO, Cab. 109–11, DRC 14, 28 February 1934.

58 See Chapter 4 below.

59 Gustav Hilger and R. Meyer, *The Incompatible Allies*, London 1954; John Erickson, *The Soviet High Command*, London 1962, pp. 346–7.

60 Erickson, *passim*.

61 Churchill College Cambridge, Christie Papers, 180/1/21; Karl Spalcke, 'Gespräche in Moskau. Die Reichswehr und die riote Armee im Jahre 1936', *Gegenwart*, 13, 1958; Herman Teske (ed.), *Profile bedeutende Soldaten*; *General Ernst Koestring*, Frankfurt 1969, pp. 94–106, denies all German military involvement with the Russians but reports interesting Russian military contacts in 1935 and 1936, pp. 85, 126.

62 *Foreign and Commonwealth Office Library*, German Foreign Ministry Photostats, Serial 1907H/429293–99.

63 As argued by Erickson, pp. 433–6.

64 Erickson, pp. 470–71, 478–9, 505–6.

65 On the Soviet maneouvres of 1937 see Gottfried Niedhart, 'Der Bündniswert der Soviet union in Urteil Grossbritanniens, 1936–1939', *Militärgeschichtliche Mitteilungen*, 2/1971.

66 See for example Frederick Wilham Winterbotham, *Secret and Personal*, London 1969.

67 Winterbotham, *op. cit.*

Chapter 3

1 Gerhard Förster, *Totalen Krieg und Blitzkrieg*, Berlin 1967, pp. 83–4.

2 Robin Higham, *The Military Intellectuals in Britain, 1918–1939*, New Brunswick, N.J. 1966, pp. 85–6.

3 Bankwitz, pp. 40–42 and the sources there cited; General André Beaufre, 'Liddell Hart and the French Army' in Michael Howard (ed.) *The Theory and Practice of War*, London 1965, pp. 134–5.

4 Heinz Guderian, *Panzer Leader*, New York 1956, p. 10.

5 Published in 1925. See Higham, *Military Intellectuals*, p. 86.

6 General Sir Frederick Pile, 'Liddell Hart and the British Army, 1919–1939' in Howard, *Theory and Practice of War*, pp. 175–176.

7 Pile, 'Liddell Hart', *op. cit.*

8 Robert J. O'Neill, 'Doctrine and Training in the German Army, 1919–1939' in Howard, *Theory and Practice of War*, pp. 148–150.

9 O'Neill, 'Doctrine and Training', pp. 150–51.

10 General von Blomberg's report of 1928 is in *Foreign and*

Commonwealth Office Library Collection, 9480/276183–236. See J. Erickson, *The Soviet High Command*, p. 270.

11 Erickson, pp. 316–17.

12 *Lectures on F.S.R. III (Operations between Armoured Forces)*, London 1932; Higham, *Military Intellectuals*, p. 72

13 *Sherman*, London 1929; Higham, *Military Intellectuals*, pp. 89–92.

14 Erickson, pp. 269–70, 350.

15 O'Neill, 'Doctrine and Training', pp. 154–6.

16 ibid., p. 157.

17 ibid., pp. 159–60.

18 ibid., pp. 160–61.

19 ibid., pp. 162–3.

20 Erickson, pp. 350–52.

21 ibid., pp. 487–9.

22 ibid., pp. 458–9.

23 ibid., pp. 508, 735, note 21, p. 770.

24 General Paul-Émile Tournoux, *Haut Commandement, Gouvernement et Défense des Frontières*, Paris 1960, p. 286.

25 Bankwitz, p. 143; R. H. S. Stolffi, 'Equipment for France in 1940', *History*, 55, 1969–70.

26 Karl Heinz Völker, *Die deutsche Luftwaffe 1933–1939*, Stuttgart 1967, pp. 30–33, 72–5.

27 M. Weygand, 'L'armée d'aujourd'hui', *Revue des Deux Mondes*, XIV, May 1938, cited in Robert J. Young, 'Preparations for Defeat: French war doctrine in the inter-war period', *Journal of European Studies*, 2, 1972.

28 Tournoux, pp. 56–67; Judith M. Hughes, *To the Maginot Line*, Cambridge, Mass., 1971; Tournoux, 'Origines de la ligne Maginot', *Revue d'Histoire de la deuxième Guerre Mondiale*, 9, 1959.

29 Stolffi, 'Equipment for France'; Jean-Marie d'Hoop, 'La politique française du réarmament (1933–1939)', *Revue d'Histoire de la deuxième Guerre Mondiale*, 4, 1954.

30 Young, 'Preparations'; Bankwitz, p. 123.

31 Liddell Hart, *The Defence of Britain*, London 1939, p. 105.

32 e.g. Tom Wintringham, *Armies of Freemen*, London 1940: *New Ways of War*, London 1940: *People's War*, London 1942.

33 *Vers l'Armée de la Métier*, Paris 1934; see also Arthur Robertson, *La doctrine de Guerre du Général de Gaulle*, Paris 1954, pp. 31–156; Bankwitz, p. 154.

34 D. C. Watt, 'Sir Warren Fisher and British Rearmament' in *Personalities and Policies*, London 1965.

35 Basil Collier, *The Defence of the United Kingdom*, London 1951.

36 Stolffi, 'Equipment'; P. le Goyet, 'Evolution de la doctrine d'emploi de l'Aviation française entre 1919 et 1939', *Revue d'Histoire de la deuxième Guerre Mondiale*, 73, 1969.

37 Erickson, pp. 500–501.

38 Sir Charles Webster and Noble Frankland, *The Strategic Bombing Offensive*, London 1961, vol. I, pp. 91–7.

39 Webster and Frankland, vol. I, p. 100.

40 National Library of Scotland, *Haldane Papers*, MS 5916, folio 104, Richmond to Haldane, 26 April 1924.

41 P. K. Kemp, *Fleet Air Arm*, London 1954, pp. 109–12.

42 ibid., p. 127.

43 M. M. Postan, D. Hay and J. D. Scott, *Design and Development of Weapons*, London 1964, pp. 308–10.

44 Robert Jungk, *Brighter than a Thousand Suns*, London, Pelican Edition 1964, p. 52.

45 *Nature*, 143, February 1939.

46 Jungk, p. 81.

47 Jungk, p. 82.

48 Margaret Gowing, *Britain and Atomic Energy 1939–1945*, London 1964, pp. 28–54.

49 Gowing, Appendix 4 and 8, pp. 439–40, 447.

Chapter 4

1 I. F. Clarke, *Voices Prophesying War 1765–1984*, Oxford 1966.

2 PRO, CP 311(23).

3 Bankwitz, p. 49.

4 PRO, CID 1082–8.

5 PRO, Cab. 19(32)2.

6 *Documents on British Foreign Policy*, Second Series, vol. V, Documents Nos 277, 284, 302, 312. Ministère des Affaires Etrangères, *Documents Diplomatiques Français, 1932–39*, 1ᵉ Serie, Tome IV, No. 82.

7 DBFP, Second Series, vol. VI, Doc. No. 395 Enclosure.

8 Tournoux, pp. 78–89.

9 See the map in Tournoux between pp. 72 and 73.
10 cited in Tournoux, p. 79.
11 ibid., p. 81.
12 ibid., pp. 260–75.
13 d'Hoop, 'La politique française du réarmament (1933–1939)', *Revue d'Histoire de la deuxième Guerre Mondiale*, 4, 1954.
14 ibid.
15 Tournoux, p. 240.
16 Tournoux, p. 265.
17 Georges Castellan, *Le Réarmament Clandestin du Reich 1930–1935*, Paris 1954, pp. 503–5.
18 Tournoux, p. 252.
19 Tournoux, p. 248.
20 Tournoux, pp. 251–6.
21 PRO, Interim Report by Minister for the Co-ordination of Defence, 15 December 1937. CP 316(37).
22 Imperial War Conference 1917: Minutes of Proceedings.
23 Richmond to Haldane, 24 June 1923, *Haldane Papers*, MS S916, folio 116.
24 James Eayrs, *In Defence of Canada*, vol. I, *From the Great War to the Great Depression*, Toronto 1964, pp. 70–75.
25 W. Hancock and M. Gowing, *British War Economy*, London 1959, p. 55.
26 M. Howard, *The Continental Commitment*, London 1972, pp. 114–15; CP 326(36), CP 334(36); Keith Feiling, *The Life of Neville Chamberlain*, London 1946, p. 314; D. C. Watt, 'Sir Warren Fisher' in *Personalities and Policies*, London 1965.
27 On the DRC see Howard, *Continental Commitment*, pp. 105–109, 113; Peter Dennis, *Decision by Default*, London 1972, pp. 35–44, 58–60; PRO, Cab. 109–111, Series DRC *passim*; Watt, 'Sir Warren Fisher . . .', *Personalities and Policies*.
28 Watt, 'Britain, the United States and Japan in 1934', Essay 4 in *Personalities and Policies*, London 1965.
29 PRO, CP 205(34), Cab. 24/250.
30 *DBFP*, 2nd Series, vol. XII, Document No. 64, Note 1; Belgium, Ministère des Affaires Etrangères, *Documents Diplomatiques Belge, 1920–1940*, vol. III, Nos 130–32; Baron von Zuylen, *Les Mains Libres, Politique Extérieure de la Belgique, 1914–1940*, Brussels 1950, pp. 293–314.
31 PRO, German Rearmament Committee report of 26 November 1934, CP 265(34), CP 268(34), CID 266th Meeting (3).
32 PRO, CP 26(36), Cab. 24(259).

33 PRO, Procés-Verbal, F.O. 371/19904, C3422/4/18; *DDF*, *1932–1939*, 2ᵉ Serie (1936–1938), Tome III, No. 97.

34 PRO, DP (P) 12.

35 Higham, *Military Intellectuals*, pp. 100–101.

36 Lawrence V. Pratt, 'The Strategic Element in Britain's Policy in the East Mediterranean, 1936–1939', London PhD Thesis 1972; Norman A. Rose, *Gentile Zionists. A Study in Anglo-Zionist Diplomacy 1929–1939*, London 1973, pp. 97–121; Michael J. Cohen, 'British Strategy and the Palestine Question, 1936–1939', *J. Contemporary History*, 7, 1972.

37 PRO, CP 26(58), Cab. 23/92.

38 PRO, DP (P) 22.

39 PRO, CID 319 Meeting, 11 April 1938.

40 Lawrence Pratt 'The Anglo-American Naval Conversations on the Far East of January 1938', *International Affairs*, 47, 1971.

41 *DGFP*, Series D, vol. I, No. 19.

42 German Naval Archives, P6 31039 'Die Marinepolitische Entwicklung 1929 bis Kriegbeginn 1939', Studie der historischen Abteilung der Marine.

43 See Gerhard Meinck, *Hitler und die deutsche Aufrüstung*, Wiesbaden 1959, pp. 9 ff.

44 *Foreign and Commonwealth Office Library*, German Naval Archives, 9945/E696011–13, 'Operative Weisung des Chefs der Marineleitung', 11 April 1931.

45 Thilo Vogelsang, 'Neue Dokumente zur Geschichte der Reichswehr, 1930–1933', *Vierteljahresheft für Zeitgeschichte*, 2, 1954, No. 8, General Liebmann Memorandum, 3 February 1933.

46 Erich Raeder, *Mein Leben*, Tübingen 1956, vol. I, p. 282.

47 Blomberg 'Weisung für die Wehrmacht im Falle von Sancktionen', 25 October 1933, *FCO Library Collection* 9945/E696978–76. The document bears the typed date '25.10.1931' but the signature makes it clear there is a typist's error, as do the marginalia.

48 Blomberg to Fritsch, 3 May 1934, *FCO Library Collection*, 9930/E694817.

49 Admiral Guse for Admiral Raeder, 9 October 1934, *FCO Library Collection*, 9945/E696022–33.

50 General Reichenau Memorandum of 12 March 1935, *FCO Library Collection*, 9945/E696061.

51 Reichenau Memorandum of 30 March 1935, *FCO Library Collection*, 9945/696052–53.

52 Blomberg manuscript memorandum, 2 May 1935, *FCO Library Collection*, 9945/E696066–69.

53 Blomberg memorandum, 11 June 1936, *FCO Library Collection* 9930/E694818–19.

54 Blomberg instruction, 2 March 1936, *FCO Library Collection*, 9944/E695938–40.

55 German Naval Archives, PG 33275, US Navy Film Tambach T.90A.

56 Bullitt to Hull, 18 May 1936, *Foreign Relations of the United States, 1936*, vol. I, pp. 300–303.

57 For the text see *DGFP*, Series C, vol. IV, Document No. 490. Nuremberg Documents. N1–4955.

58 Nuremberg Documents, 175–C.

59 See *DGFP*, Series D, vol. VII, Appendix K, Document No. (i).

Chapter 5

1 Georg Thomas, *Geschichte der deutschen Wehr-und Rüstungs Wirtschaft (1918–1943/45)*, Boppard am Rhein 1966, p. 3.

2 ibid., p. 51.

3 ibid.

4 W. N. Medlicott, *The Economic Blockade*, London 1952, vol. I, pp. 12–13.

5 J. D. Scott and R. Hughes, *The Administration of British War Production*, London 1955, p. 53.

6 Medlicott, p. 13.

7 See, for example, the entries from Neville Chamberlain's diary of 1933 cited by Ian Macleod, *Neville Chamberlain*, London 1961, p. 174 and by Keith Feiling, *The Life of Neville Chamberlain*, London 1946, p. 226.

8 See for example, F. D. Roosevelt to Fred I. Kent, 22 May 1934, in Edgar B. Nixon (ed.), *Franklin D. Roosevelt and Foreign Affairs*, Cambridge, Mass. 1969, p. 119.

9 PRO, CP 24(38).

10 Cab. Cons. 5(38).

11 CP 247(38) Appendix to Annex I.

12 CP 316(37).

13 See *DGFP*, Series D, vol. I, Nos 65, 70, 71, 72.

14 Miles (pseudonym for Herbert Rosinski), *Deutschlands Kriegs-*

bereitschaft und Kriegsaussichten, Zurich 1939, pp. 125–7. For a rather fuller version of Brinckman's breakdown which does not, however, mention his Cologne speech see Hans Kehrl, *Krisenmanager im Dritten Reich*, Düsseldorf 1973, pp. 145–55.

15 Justus Schmidt in *Kriegswirtschaftlichen Jahresberichte*, 1937, cited Miles, p. 32; see ibid, pp. 25–35.

16 Malcolm Muggeridge (ed.), *Ciano's Diary 1939–1943*, London 1947, entry of 18 September 1939.

17 *Ciano's Diary 1939–1943*, entry of 19 February 1939.

18 ibid., entries of 24 and 25 August 1939.

19 See German Naval Archives, PG 33744, reports of 3, 10, 19, 26 October, 7 November 1939; DGFP, Series D, vol. IV, No. 402; German Naval Archives, *FCO Library Collection*, M70/M002256–57, Admiral Guse Minute 21 October 1939.

20 *DGFP*, Series D, vol. IV, Nos 403, 406.

21 Colonel P. Le Goyet, 'Evolution de la doctrine d'emploi de l'aviation française entre 1919 et 1939', *Revue d'Histoire de la deuxième Guerre Mondiale*, 73, 1969.

22 John McVickers Haight Jr, *American Aid to France, 1938–1940*, New York 1970, pp. 3–9; see also the same, 'les Negociations Françaises pour la fourniture d'Avions Américains, Ière partie – avant Munich', *Forces Aériennes Françaises*, 198, 1963.

23 General Georges Gamelin, *Servir*, Paris 1946, vol. II, pp. 322–331.

24 ibid.

25 Gamelin, vol. II, p. 334.

26 Gamelin, vol. III, pp. 26–32.

27 PRO, Report on visit to French manoeuvres, November 1937, FO371/20732.

28 R. J. Minney, *The Private Papers of Hore-Belisha*, London 1960, pp. 120–21.

29 Gamelin, vol. II, p. 346.

30 On Faucher see *DBFP*, 3rd series, vol. I, Documents Nos 428, 502; *Les Evénements Survenus en France, Témoignages*, vol. V, pp. 1200 ff for Faucher's own evidence.

31 Paul Stehlin, *Témoignage pour l'Histoire*, Paris 1964, pp. 89–92.

32 *The Wartime Journals of Charles A. Lindbergh*, New York 1970, entry of 1 October 1938.

33 Robert J. Young, 'French Policy and the Munich Crisis of 1938', Canadian Historical Association, *Historical Papers 1970*, pp. 186–206.

34 Gamelin, vol. II, p. 358; Vuillemin to Guy La Chambre, *Les Evénements Survenus en France, Témoignages*, vol. II, p. 313.
35 Gamelin, vol. I, pp. 124–30.
36 Gamelin, vol. II, pp. 389–401.
37 *DBFP*, 3rd Series, vol. III, No. 325, Cab. 45/13.
38 For the British record see DP(P) 56 Annex I. See also Sir John Kennedy, *The Business of War*, London 1951, p. 8. For the French view see J. Lecuir et P. Fridenson, 'L'organisation de la co-operation aérienne Franco-britannique (1935–Mai 1940)', *Revue d'Histoire de la deuxième Guerre Mondiale*, 73, 1969.
39 'Protocols of the Polish–French General Staffs Conference in Paris, May 1939', *Bellona*, II, 1958. Waclaw Jedrzejewicz (ed.), *Diplomat in Paris 1936–1939, Memoirs of Juliusz Lukasiewicz, Ambassador of Poland*, New York 1970, pp. 210–23.
40 Gamelin, vol. II, pp. 426–7.
41 *Lukasiewicz, Memoirs*, pp. 313 ff.; Nicholas Bethell, *The War Hitler Won*, London 1973, *passim*.
42 André Beaufre, *1940 The Fall of France*, London 1967, p. 119.
43 *Les Evénements Survenus en France*, Rapport, Tome II, pp. 276–8.
44 Paxton, *Parades and Politics*, p. 66.
45 ibid.
46 *DGFP*, Series D, vol. II, Documents Nos 132, 133. See also D. C. Watt, 'Hitler's Visit to Rome and the May Week-end Crisis', *J. Contemporary History*, 1974.
47 *DGFP*, Series D, vol. II, Document No. 175; Watt, 'Hitler's Visit to Rome . . .'; D. C. Watt, 'The May Crisis of 1938, A rejoinder to Mr Wallace', *Slavonic and East European Review*, XLIV, 1966.
48 Watt, 'Hitler's Visit to Rome . . .'; Watt, 'The May Crisis . . .'.
49 *DGFP*, Series D, vol. IV, Document No. 411.
50 *DGFP*, Series D, vol. VI, Documents Nos 149, 185. ND—120–C; see also M. Zgorniak, 'Les préparatifs de l'attaque contre la Pologne', *Revue d'Histoire de la deuxième Guerre Mondiale*, 77, 1970.
51 *DGFP*, Series D, vol. II, Document No. 433, ND—70–L.
52 Foerster, *Generaloberst Ludwig Beck*, pp. 100–105; Buchheit, *Beck*, pp. 133–8; Müller, pp. 301–3.
53 Max Domarus, *Hitler, Reden und Proklamationen 1932–1945*, Munich 1965, vol. I, pp. 868–9; Müller, pp. 307–9.
54 *DGFP*, Series D, vol. II, Document No. 221, ND 388–PS.
55 Müller, pp. 309–12.

56 Müller, pp. 335–7.

57 Domarus, vol. I, pp. 880–81; Müller, pp. 338–9.

58 ND 647–PS; Domarus, vol. I, pp. 881–2; *DBFP*, 3rd Series, vol. II, Nos 631, 658.

59 *DBFP*, 3rd Series, vol. II, Appendix IV *passim*; Bobo Scheurig, *Ewald von Kleist-Schmenzin; ein Konservative gegen Hitler*, Oldenbourg 1968, pp. 150–60.

60 *DBFP*, 3rd Series, vol. I, Nos 510–11; *DGFP*, D, Appendix III(H) *passim*; Franz Wiedemann, *Der Mann der Feldherr werden wollte*, Hann 1964, pp. 158–67.

61 Domarus, vol. II, p. 1075; Müller, p. 383.

62 *DBFP*, 3rd Series, vol. V, Appendix I, No. (x); vol. VI, Nos 269, 277, 372; vol. VII, No. 138; Churchill College, Cambridge, Admiral T. H. Godfrey draft memoirs.

63 *DBFP*, 3rd Series, vol. IV, Nos 5, 8, 18, 20, 26, 27, 28, 29, 30, 39, 40, 41, 45, 48, 49, 50, 51, 54, 55, 57, 58, 64, 70, 72, 75, 77, 80, 81, 87, 88, 94, 98, 99, 101, 102; *Documents Diplomatiques Belges, 1920–1940*, Tome V, Nos 50–56; *F.R.U.S., 1939*, vol. I, pp. 2–7, 9; David Dilks (ed.), *The Diaries of Sir Alexander Cadogan, 1938–1945*, London 1971, entries of 17, 19, 23, 25 and 26 January 1939; *The Diplomatic Diaries of Oliver Harvey, 1937–1940*, London 1970, entries of 24, 26, 29 January 1939.

64 Ian Colvin, *Vansittart: A Study in Statecraft*, London 1965, pp. 303–311.

65 Donald McLachlan, *Room 39*, London 1968; pp. 244–6; *Cadogan Diaries*, entry of 3 April 1939.

66 On this episode see Winifred Baumgart, 'Zur Ansprache Hitlers vor den Führern der Wehrmacht im August 1939', *Vierteljahresheft für Zeitgeschichte*, 16, 1968.

67 Lord Ismay, *Memoirs*, London 1960, pp. 77–8; Sir Leslie Hollis, *One Marine's Tale*, London 1956, pp. 49–51: Churchill College, Cambridge, *Hankey Papers*, Hankey to Robin Hankey, 3 April 1938.

68 Minney, p. 69, Hore-Belisha to Chamberlain, November 1937.

69 CID 1394 and 1394–B, COS 68 Cab. 24/274, 4 February 1938.

70 PRO, FO 371/21593, Eden to Chamberlain, 1 January 1938, also in PREM 1/276.

71 See Hankey's memoranda of 1937 on Italy in Cab. 63/52.

72 CID 1366–B.

73 DP(P)22.

74 CID 1487–B.

75 CP 3(39).

76 CP 28(39), Cab. Cons. 5(39); CP 49(39), Cab. Cons. 8(39).

77 DP(P), 44.

78 Peter Dennis, *Decision by Default*, London 1972, pp. 206 ff. See also the British Inst. of Public Opinion's polls on the issue of conscription, 1937–1939 printed in *Public Opinion Quarterly*, March 1940.

79 See the memoirs of the members of the Field Security Police stationed in France in 1940; Sir Basil Bartlett, *My First War*, London 1940; A. Gwynn-Browne, *FSP*, London 1942.

80 Sir John Wheeler-Bennett, *The Nemesis of Power*, London 1953, p. 458.

81 Herman Graml, 'Der Fall Oster', *Vierteljahresheft für Zeitgeschichte*, 14, 1966.

82 Otto John, *Twice through the Lines*, London 1972; *Zweimal kam ich heim*, Düsseldorf 1969.

83 David Astor, 'Why the revolt against Hitler was ignored', *Encounter*, XXXII, 1969.

Chapter 6

1 Bankwitz, p. 293. The order, *Ordre Général d'Opérations* No. 1 was dated 22 May.

2 On the significance of this see Bankwitz, pp. 293–305.

3 R. H. S. Stolffi, 'Equipment for Victory in France in 1940', *History*, 55, 1970.

4 Paxton, pp. 71–93.

5 Paxton, pp. 136–7.

6 Paul Marie de la Gorce, pp. 344–6; Paxton, p. 414.

7 Paxton, pp. 51–4.

8 Paxton, pp. 378–80.

9 Raoul Girardet (ed.), *La Crise Militaire Française 1945–1962*, Paris 1962, p. 21.

10 Paxton, pp. 417–18, 420.

11 F. W. Deakin, *The Brutal Friendship*, London 1962, p. 12.

12 M. G. Warner, 'Politique d'Italie a l'égard de la Grèce et de la Yougoslavie' in *La Guerre en Mediterranée 1939–1945*, Actes du Colleque International tenu a Paris du 8 au 11 Avril 1969,

Paris 1971, pp. 513–34, Martin von Crefeld, *Hitler's Strategy 1940–1941, The Balkan Clue*, Cambridge 1973, pp. 18–26, 56–7.

13 Alan Moorehead, *Montgomery*, London 1946, p. 141.

14 Alan Moorehead, *The End in Africa*, London 1943, p. 205.

15 Cited in Deakin, p. 283.

16 Friedrich Karl von Plehwe, *The End of an Alliance*, London 1971, pp. 67–8, 97.

17 Giampaolo Pansa, *L'Esercito di Salò*, Milan 1969, *passim*.

18 Müller, p. 242 quoting Keitel.

19 Müller, pp. 343–4.

20 Harold Deutsch, *The Conspiracy against Hitler in the Twilight War*, London 1968, *passim*.

21 cf. D. C. Watt, 'Les alliés et la résistance allemande', *Revue d'Histoire de la deuxième Guerre Mondiale*, 36, 1959.

22 See the somewhat sensational account of this in Ladislas Farrago, *The Game of the Foxes*, London 1972, pp. 121–9.

23 Walter Z. Laqueur, *Russia and Germany*, London 1971, pp. 272–3.

24 Wolfgang Leonhard, *A Child of the Revolution*, London 1957, pp. 280-338.

25 Charles de Gaulle, *War Memoirs; Salvation 1944–1946: Documents*, London 1960, pp. 83–105; K. Tsybina, 'The German Question and Wartime Franco–Soviet Relations, 1941–45', *International Affairs* (Moscow), April 1959, pp. 122–48.

26 cf. Walter Lipgers (ed.), *Europa-Föderationspläne der Widerstandsbewegungen, 1940–1945*, Munich 1968, especially chapter 2.

27 *Trial of the Major War Criminals before the International Military Tribunal*, Nuremberg 1948, vol. XXII, pp. 522–3.

28 cf. Christopher J. Bartlett, *The Long Retreat*, London 1972; Richard N. Rosecrance, *Defence of the Realm, British Strategy in the Nuclear Epoch*, London 1968.

29 D. C. Watt, 'The Decision to Withdraw from the Gulf. A Study in Irrelevancy', *Political Quarterly*, 1968.

30 Bartlett, *The Long Retreat*, p. 21.

31 Paxton, p. 421.

32 Jean Planchais, *Une Histoire Politique de l'Armée 1940–1967*, Paris 1967.

33 Gerhard Wettig, *Entmilitarisierung und Wiederbewaffnung in Deutschland 1943–1955*, Munich 1967, pp. 221–4, 289-301.

34 cf. Carl-Gerö von Ilsemann, *Die Bundeswehr in der Demokratie Zeit der inneren Führung*, Hamburg 1971.
35 Wettig, *op. cit.* See also M. Donald Hancock, *The Bundeswehr and the National People's Army: A Comparative Study of German Civil-Military Policy*, Denver, Colorado, 1972.

Select Bibliography

1 *Unpublished Sources*

At the moment of writing the only major official military archives in Europe open to historical research are those of Great Britain and that section of pre-1945 German military archives which fell into the hands of the Western allies in 1945 and was eventually returned to the West German authorities and now forms part of the *Bundesarchiv* in Koblenz. A very considerable volume of German military records were microfilmed during their stay in the United States. The microfilms are catalogued and may be purchased from the US National Archives. A smaller volume of German naval records were photostated and the photostats deposited with those of the German Foreign Ministry archives in the Foreign Office Library. The French military archives suffered considerably in the holocaust of June 1940, and are gradually being made accessible to academic historians up to the years 1938–9. So far as I am aware, there is only very limited access to the Italian military archives. A small quantity of Italian military records was also microfilmed by the United States authorities and copies deposited in the US National Archives. Of private papers, Britain has by far the largest range of collections, including those of Air Marshal Sir Robert Brooke-Popham, Admiral Lord Chatfield, Colonel Christie, Admiral Lord Cunningham, Admiral Drax, Lord Hankey, General Sir Percy Hobart, Lord Ismay, General Lord Ironside, Admiral Lord Keyes, Captain Sir Basil Liddell Hart, General Mason-Macfarlane, General Percival, General Peake, Lord Swinton and Lord Weir, to name only a few, mainly concentrated in five big repositories: Kings College, London, Military Archives; Churchill College Library, Cambridge; Imperial War Museum; National Maritime Museum and the British Museum.

2 *Official Histories*

FRANCE

Ministère des Armées—État-major de l'armée de terre:

Francis André Paoli, *L'armée française de 1919 à 1939: la reconversion*, Paris n.d.

L'armée française de 1919 à 1939: la phase de fermeté 1920–1924, Paris n.d.

Général Jean Bernachot, *Les armées françaises en Orient aprés l'armistice de 1918*: vol. 1: *L'armée française: d'Orient: l'armée de Hongrie*, Paris 1970; vol. II: *l'armée du Danube*, Paris 1970; vol. III: *Le corps d'occupation de Constantinople*, Paris 1972

Guerre 1939–1945: Les grandes unités françaises; Histoire succincts; Campagnes de Tunisie et d'Italie; Opérations de Corse et de l'Île d'Elbe, Paris 1970

Colonel Pierre le Goyet, *La participation française à la campagne d'Italie, 1943–44*, Paris 1969

Lieutenant-Colonel Georges Boult, *Le corps expéditionnaire français en Italie: la campagne d'hiver*, Paris 1971

GREAT BRITAIN

Cabinet Office, *History of the Second World War*, Civil Series:

W. K. Hancock and M. Gowing, *British War Economy*, London 1949

W. N. Medlicott, *The Economic Blockade*, vol. I, London 1954

T. H. O'Brien, *Civil Defence*, London 1955

M. M. Postan, *British War Production*, London 1952

M. M. Postan, D. Hay and J. D. Scott, *Design and Development of Weapons*, London 1964

Cabinet Office, *History of the Second World War*, Military Series:

Basil Collier, *The Defence of the United Kingdom*, London 1951

Sir Charles Webster and Noble Frankland, *The Strategic Air Offensive against Germany*, vols I–IV, London 1961

(Only those volumes of these two series are listed which bear on the pre-1939 period.)

ITALY

Guiseppe Santoro, *L'Aeronautica Italiana nella seconda Guerra Mondiale*, Rome 1957

Ministero della Difesa, Stato Maggiore dell'Esercito, Ufficio Storica: *In Africa Settentrionale, La Preparazione al Conflitto; L'Avanzata Sidi el Barrani (Ottobre 1935–Settembre 1940)* Rome 1955

Maresciallo d'Italia Giovanni Mesi, *Il Ia armata Italiane in Tunisia*, Rome 1950

Generale di Corpo Armata Vittorio Sogno, *Il XXX Corpo d'Armata Italiano in Tunisia*, Rome 1952

Colonel Salvatore Ernesto Crapanzano, *Il I Raggruppiemento Motorizzato Italiano (1943–1944)*, Rome 1949

La Prima Offensiva Britannica in Africa Settentrionale (Ottobre 1940–Febbraio 1941), 2 vols, Rome, n.d.

Seconda Offensiva Britannica in Africa Settentrionale e Repiegamento Italo–Tedesco nella Sirtica Orientale (18 Novembre 1941–17 Gennaio 1942), 2 vols, Rome 1949

Tezza Offensiva Britannica in Africa Settentrionale—La Battaglia di el Alamein e il Repiegamento in Tunisia (6 Settembre 1942–4 Febbraio 1943), 2 vols, Rome 1961

Marina Militare—Ufficio Storico, *La Marina Italiana nella seconda guerra mondiale*, 18 vols, Rome 1952 in progress

Ministero degli Affari Esteri: Comitalo per la documentazione dell'opera dell'Italia in Africa: l'Italia in Africa, Serio Storico Militare vol I: *L'opera dell'esercito, 1885–1943* Tomo I: *Ordinamento a reclutamento*, by Massimo Adolfo Vitale, Rome 1960

vol. I, Tomo II: *Avvenimenti militario e impiego Pt. I: Africa Orientale 1868–1934* by M. A. Vitale, Rome 1962

vol. I, Tomo III: *Avvenimenti militarie e impiego Africa settentrionali (1911–1943)* by M. A. Vitale, Rome 1962

vol. II: *L'opera della marina (1868–1943)* by Giuseppe Fioravanzo e Guido Viti, Rome 1959

vol. III: *L'opera dell'aeronautica.* Tomo I *Eritrea–Libya (1918–1932)* by Vincenzo Lioy, Rome 1964

vol. III, Tomo II: *Eritrea, Somalia, Etiopia (1919–1937)* by V. Lioy, Rome 1964

vol. IV: *I Corpi armati con funzioni civili* by M. A. Vitale and others, Rome 1962

3 *Trials, Enquiries, etc.*

The exigencies of defeat produced war crimes, trials and parliamentary enquiries in France, Germany and Italy. Their historical value is clouded by the normal disadvantages of the adversary process of enquiry, but the range of documentation and testimony makes these essential reading for the historian.

GERMANY

Trial of the Major War Criminals before the International Military Tribunal, 42 vols (Nuremberg 1948)
Trials of War Criminals, (Washington D.C. 1950)
vol. II, *Case 2, The US v Erhard Milch*
vols X, XI, *Case 12, The US v. von Leeb et al.*

FRANCE

Les evénements survenus en France de 1933 à 1945; Témoignages et documents recueillis par la commission d'enquête parlementaire, 9 vols
Rapport de M. Charles Serre, deputé en nom de la commission d'enquête parlementaire, 2 vols, Paris 1947–51
Maurice Ribet, *Le Procès de Riom*, Paris 1945
Procès du Marechal Pétain, Paris 1945

ITALY

Processo Graziani, 2 vols, Rome 1949

4 *Memoirs, Diaries and Biographies*

Quirino Armellini, *Diario di Guerra: Nova Mesi al Commando Supremo*, Rome 1948
Général J. Armengaud, *Batailles politiques et militaires sur l'Europe, Témoignages (1932–1940)*, Paris 1948
P. Badoglio, *L'Italia nella Seconda Guerra Mondiale*, Milan 1946
Philip C. Bankwitz, *Maxime Weygand and Civil-Military Relations in Modern France*, Cambridge, Mass. 1967

Général André Beaufre, *1940 The Fall of France*, London 1967
translation of *Le Drame de 1940*, Paris 1965

Paolo Berardi, *Memorie di un Capo di Stato Maggiore dell'Esercito*,
Bologna 1954

P. Billotte, *Le temps des armes*, Paris 1972

Lord Birkenhead, *The Prof. in Two Worlds*, London 1961

B. Bond (ed.), *Chief of Staff: The Diaries of Lieutenant General
Sir Henry Pownall*: vol. I, *1933–1940*, London 1972

Peter Bor, *Gespräche mit Halder*, Wiesbaden 1950

Andrew Boyle, *Trenchard*, London 1962

Gert Bucheit, *Ludwig Beck*, Munich 1964

Emilio Canevari, *La Guerra Italiana*, 2 vols, Rome 1948

Ugo Cavallero, *Commando Supremo, Diario 1940–43*, Bologna
1948

E. Caviglia, *Diario, Aprile 1925–Marza 1945*, Rome 1952

W. S. Chalmers, *Life and Letters of David, Earl Beatty*, London
1951
Full Cycle: the biography of Sir David Home Ramsay, London
1959

Lord Chatfield, *It Might Happen Again*, London 1947

Basil Collier, *Brasshat*, London 1961
Dowding: Leader of the Few, London 1967

J. R. Colville, *Gort: Man of Valour*, London 1972

Alain Darlan, *Darlan parle*, Paris 1952

Lord Douglas, *The Years of Command*, London 1966

Sir Basil Embry, *Mission Completed*, London 1957

C. Favagrosso, *Perche perdemmo la Guerra*, Milan 1947

Bernard Fergusson, *Wavell: Portrait of a Soldier*, London 1961

Professor Wolfgang Foerster, *Generaloberst Ludwig Beck, sein
Kampf gegen den Krieg*, Munich 1953

Adolf Galland, *The First and the Last*, London 1957

Général Maurice Gamelin, *Servir*, 3 vols, Paris 1946–7

Général Maurice Henri Gauché, *Le deuxième bureau en travail,
1935–1940*, Paris 1954

Otto Gessler, *Reichswehrpolitik in der Weimarer Zeit*, Stuttgart
1958

Geyr von Schweppenburg, *The Critical Years*, London 1952

Walter Görlitz, *Generalfeldmarschall Keitel: Verbrecher oder
Offizier*, Göttingen 1961

R. Graziani, *Io ho difeso la Patria*, Milan 1948

Dorothea Groener-Geyer, *General Groener, Soldat und Staatsmann*,
Frankfurt 1955

Helmut Groscurth, *Tagebücher eines Abwehroffiziers, 1938–1940*, Stuttgart 1970

Heinz Guderian, *Panzer Leader* (London 1952) translation of *Erinnerungen eines Soldaten*, Heidelberg 1950

Francis de Guingand, *Operation Victory*, London 1947

Franz Halder, *Der Kriegstagebuch; tägliche Aufzeichnungen des Chefs du Generalstabes des Heeres 1939–1942*, Stuttgart 1962 *Hitler als Feldherr*, Munich 1949

Colonel Sir Charles Harington, *Tim Harington Looks Back*, London 1940

Adolf Heusinger, *Befehl im Widerstreit*, Stuttgart 1950

Sir Leslie Hollis, *One Marine's Tale*, London 1956

Sir Leslie Hollis and James Leasor, *War at the Top*, London 1959

Friedrich Hossbach, *Zwischen Wetounacht und Hitler 1934–38*, Wolfenbülke 1949

Lord Ironside, *High Road to Command: the Diaries of Major-General Sir Edmund Ironside 1920–1922*, London 1972

Lord Ismay, *Memoirs*, London 1960

W. Keitel, *Memoirs*, New York 1966

Sir John Kennedy, *The Business of War*, London 1951

A. Kesselring, *Soldat bis zum letzten Tag*, Bonn 1953

[Ernst Koestring] Hermann Teske (ed.), *Profile bedeutender Soldaten General Ernst Koestring; der militärische Mittler zwischen den deutschen Reich und der Sowjetunion 1921–1941*, Frankfurt am Main 1966

Sir Basil Liddell Hart, *Memoirs*, London 1965

The Wartime Journals of Charles R. Lindbergh, New York n.d., [1972]

Lord Londonderry, *Wings of Destiny*, London 1943

Bernard Lossberg, *Im Wehrmachtsführungsstab*, Hamburg 1950

Kenneth Macksey, *Armoured Crusader: A Biography of Major-General Sir Percy Hobart*, London 1967

R. Macleod and D. Kelly, *The Ironside Diaries, 1937–1940*, London 1962

Erich von Manstein, *Aus einem Soldatenleben*, Bonn 1958

Arthur Marder, *Portrait of an Admiral: the Life and Papers of Sir Herbert Richmond*, London 1952

Sir Giffard Martel, *An Outspoken Soldier*, London 1949

Jacques Minarst, *Le drame du désarmament français (Les aspects politiques et techniques) La Revanche Allemande 1918–1939*, Paris 1959

R. J. Minney (ed.), *The Private Papers of Hore-Belisha*, London 1960

Viscount Montgomery of Alamein, *Memoirs*, London 1958

J. H. Morgan, *Assize of Arms*, London 1945

Vincenz Müller, *Ich fand das wahre Vaterland*, Berlin 1963

Lady Octavia Murray, *The Making of a Civil Servant, Sir Oswyn Murray, GCB, Secretary of the Admiralty, 1917–1936*, London 1940

Sir Frederick Pile, *Ack-Ack: Britain's defence against attack during the Second World War*, London 1949

Friedrich Karl von Plehwe, *The End of an Alliance: Rome's defection from the Axis in 1943*, Oxford 1971

Freiherr von Rabenau, *Seeckt, aus seinem Leben*, Berlin 1960

Erich von Raeder, *Mein Leben*, Tübingen 1956

W. Reader, *Lord Weir, Architect of Air Power*, London 1968

Enno von Rintelen, *Mussolini als Bundesgenosse*, Tübingen 1951

M. Roatta, *Otto Milioni di Baionette*, Milan 1946

Stephen Roskill, *Hankey: Man of Secrets*, 3 vols, London 1970, 1972, 1974.

H. G. Schall-Riancour, *Aufstand und Gehorsam: Offizierstum und Generalstab im Umbruch. Leben und Wirken von Generaloberst Frank Halder, Generalstabschef 1938–1942*, Wiesbaden 1972

Sir John Slessor, *The Central Blue*, London 1956

Sir John Smyth, vc, *Percival and the tragedy of Singapore*, London 1971

Sir Edward Spears, *Assignment to Catastrophe*, 2 vols, London 1954, 1956

A. Speer, *Inside the Third Reich*, London 1970, translation of *Erinnerungen*

Paul Stehlin, *Témoignage pour l'histoire*, Paris 1964

Hermann Teske, *Des silberne Spiegel: Generalstabsdienst unter der Lupe*, Heidelberg 1962

Elizabeth Wagner (ed.), *Der General Quartiermeister: Briefe und Tagebuchanzeichnungen des Generalquartiermeister des Heeres, General Edward Wagner 1918–1941*, Munich 1963

Walter Warlimont, *Im Hauptquartier der Wehrmacht 1939–1945*, Bonn 1964

Sir Robert Watson-Watt, *Three Steps to Victory*, London 1957

Siegfried Westphal, *Heer im Fesseln*, Bonn 1950

Maxime Weygand, *Mémoires, III, Rappelé au Service*, Paris 1956

Fritz Wiedemann, *Der Mann der Feldherr werden wollte: Erlebnisse und Erfahrungen des Vorgesetzten Hitlers im Ersten Weltkrieg*, Dortmund 1964

Sir Reginald Wingate, *Lord Ismay*, London 1970

5   *Studies and Articles*

Rudolf Absolon, *Wehrgesetz und Wehrdienst 1935–1945, Das Personalwesen in der Wehrmacht*, Boppard am Rhein, 1960

Tony Albord, 'L'ére crépusculaire de la stratégie, 1919–1939', *Revue de la Défense nationale*, 1965

Karl Otmar von Aretin, 'Der Eid auf Hitler; Eine Studie zum moralischen Verfall des Offizierkorps der Reichswehr', *Politische Studien*, 7, 1957

Raymond Aron, *Peace and War: a theory of international relations*, London 1966, translation of *Paix et guerre entre les nations*, Paris 1962

G. A. J. P. Auphan and J. Mordal, *La Marine française pendant la Seconde Guerre Mondiale*, Paris 1958

Christopher John Bartlett, *The Long Retreat: A Short History of British Defence Policy, 1945–1970*, London 1971

Fabrizio di Benedetti, *Il potere militare in Italia*, Bari 1971

Rolf Benser, *Die deutsche Flottenpolitik von 1933 bis 1939*, Frankfurt 1958

W. Bernhardt, *Die deutsche Aufrüstung 1934–1939*, Frankfurt 1969

Carlo del Biase, *L'Aquila d'Oro: Storia della Stato Maggiore Italiano 1861–1945*, Milan 1969

Gerhard Biedlungmaier, 'Die strategische und operative Überlegungen der Marine', *Wehrwissenschaftliche Rundschau*, 13, 1963

Hildegard Boeninger, 'Hitler and the German Generals, 1934–1938', *J. Central European Affairs*, 14, 1954

Marc Antonio Bragadin, *Il Dramma della Marina Italiana 1940–1945*, Rome 1948

Charles Burdick, 'Die deutsche militärische Planungen gegenüber Frankreich 1933–1938' in *Wehrwissenschaftliche Rundschau*, 6, 1956

Eugène Carrias, *La pensée militaire française*, Paris 1960

F. L. Carsten, *The Reichswehr and Politics, 1918–1933*, Oxford 1966

Georges Castellan, *Le réarmament clandestin du Reich 1930–1935*, Paris 1954

Mario Cervi, *The Hollow Legions: Mussolini's blunder in Greece*, London 1972

Richard D. Challener, *The French Theory of the Nation in Arms, 1866–1939*, New York 1955

R. Chaput, *Disarmament in British Foreign Policy*, London 1935

F. Coghlan, 'Armaments, Economic Policy and Appeasement', *History*, 57, 1972

M. J. Cohen, 'British Strategy and the Palestine Question, 1936–1959', *J. Contemporary History*, 7, 1972

Gordon A. Craig, *The Politics of the Prussian Army 1640–1945*, Oxford 1955

Philip Darby, *British Defence Policy East of Suez, 1947–1968*, London 1973

Das deutsche Bild der russischen und sowjetischen Marine, Frankfurt am Main, 1962

F. W. Deakin, *The Brutal Friendship: Mussolini, Hitler and the Fall of Italian Fascism*, London 1962

Karl Demeter, *The German Officer Corps in Society and State, 1650–1945*, London 1965, translation of *Das deutsche Offizierkorps in Gesellschaft und Staat 1650–1945*, Frankfurt 1964

Peter Dennis, *Decision by Default: Peacetime Conscription and British Defence 1919–1939*, London 1972

Harold Deutsch, *The Conspiracy against Hitler in the Twilight War*, Minneapolis 1968

D. Divine, *The Broken Wing*, London 1966

J. Dülffer, *Weimar, Hitler und die Marine; Reichspolitik und Flottenbau 1920–1939*, Dusseldorf 1972

E. M. Earle (ed.), *The Makers of Modern Strategy*, Princeton, 1943

James Eayrs, *In Defence of Canada*, vol. I: *From the Great War to the Great Depression*; vol. II: *Appeasement and Rearmament*, Toronto 1963 and 1965

Waldamar Erfurth, *Die Geschichte des deutschen Generalstabs 1918–1945*, Göttingen 1957

John Erickson, *The Soviet High Command 1918–1941*, London 1962

Jean Feller, *Le dossier de l'armée française: La Guerre de Cinquante Ans 1914–1962*, Paris 1966

W. M. Flohock, *André Malraux and the Tragic Imagination*, Stanford, 1952

Gerhard Förster, *Totaler Krieg und Blitzkrieg*, Berlin 1967

Hermann Foertsch, *Schuld und Verhängnis*, Stuttgart 1951

Otto Wilhelm Forster, *Die Befestigungswesen*, Neckargermund 1960

G. Frede and Otto Schüddekopf, *Wehrmacht und Politik 1935–1945*, Hanover 1951

Carl Axell Gemsell, *Raeder, Hitler und Skandinavien: Der Kampf für einer maritimen Operationsplan*, Lund 1965

Norman H. Gibbs, *The Origins of Imperial Defence*, London 1955

Raoul Girardet, *La société militaire dans la France contemporaire, 1815–1939*, Paris 1953

Raoul Girardet (ed.), *La crise militaire française 1945–1962: aspects sociologiques et idéologiques*, Paris 1964

Avriel Goldberger, *Visions of a New Hero*, Paris 1965

Paul Marie de la Gorce, *The French Army: A military-political history*, London 1963

Harold I. Gordon Jr, *The Reichswehr and the German Republic 1919–1926*, Princeton, 1951

Walter Goerlitz, *The German General Staff 1657–1945*, London 1953, translation of *Der deutschen Generalstabs*, Frankfurt 1950

Colonel P. Le Goyet, 'Evolution de la doctrine d'emploi de l'aviation française entre 1919 et 1939' *Revue d'Histoire de la deuxième Guerre Mondiale*, 73, 1969

Helmut Greiner, *Die oberste Wehrmachtsführung 1919–1943*, Wiesbaden 1951

John M. Haight Jr, *American Aid to France 1930–1940*, New York 1970

M. Donald Hancock, *The Bundeswehr and the National People's Army: a comparative study of German civil–military policy*, Denver 1972

Robin Higham, *Armed Forces in Peacetime*, London 1962

'The Dangerously Neglected—the British Military Intellectuals, 1918–1939', *Mil. Affairs*, 29, 1965

The Military Intellectuals in Britain 1918–1939, New Brunswick, 1966

F. H. Hinsley, *Command of the Sea*, London 1950

Hitler's Strategy, London 1951

Stanley Hoffmann, 'The Effects of World War Two on French Society and Politics', *French Historical Studies*, 1963

Jean-Marie d'Hoop, 'La politique française du réarmament (1933–1939)', *Revue d'histoire de la deuxième Guerre Mondiale*, 4, 1954

Michael Howard, *The Continental Commitment*, London 1972

(ed.), *Soldiers and Governments*, London 1957

(ed.), *The Theory and Practice of War*, London 1965

Walther Hubatsch, *Der Admiralstab und die obersten Marinebehörden im Deutschland 1840–1945*, Frankfurt am Main 1962

Judith M. Hughes, *To the Maginot Line: The Politics of French Military Preparation in the 1920s*, Cambridge, Mass. 1971

Carl-Gerö von Ilsemann, *Die Bundeswehr im der Demoskratie: Zeit der inneren Führung*, Hamburg 1971

Franklin A. Johnson, *Defence by Committee*, London 1960

Robert Jungk, *Brighter than a Thousand Suns: a personal history of the atomic scientists*, London 1958

P. K. Kemp, *The Fleet Air Arm*, London 1954
Victory at Sea, 1939–1945, London 1957

Jere Klemens King, *Generals and Politicians*, Berkeley 1951
Foch versus Clemenceau, Cambridge, Mass. 1960

B. Klein, *Germany's Economic Preparations for War*, Cambridge, Mass. 1959

Asher Lee, *The Soviet Air Force*, London 1950

Sir Basil Liddell Hart, *The Other Side of the Hill*, London 1949
The Tank: the history of the Royal Tank Regiment, London 1959

Jay Luvaas, *The Education of an Army: British military thought, 1815–1940*, Chicago 1964

Les Relations Militaires Franco–Belges de Mars 1936 au Mai 1940: travaux d'un colloque d'historiens belges et français, Paris 1968

Arthur Marder, 'The Royal Navy and the Ethiopian crisis of 1935–1936', *American Historical Review*, 25, 1970

Gerhard Meinck, *Hitler und die deutsche Aufrüstung 1933–1937*, Wiesbaden 1959

Miles (pseud. Herbert Rosinski) *Deutschlands Kriegsbereitschaft und Kriegsaussichten im Spiegel der deutschen Fachliteratur*, Zurich 1939

Klaus-Jürgen Müller, *Das Heer und Hitler; Armee und National-sozialistisches Regime 1933–1940*, Stuttgart 1969

Burkhardt Müller-Hildebrand, *Das Heer 1943–1945*, Darmstadt 1954

Jacques Nobécourt and Jean Planchais, *Une histoire politique de l'armée*, vol I: *de Pétain à Pétain*; vol. II: *de Gaulle à de Gaulle*, Paris 1967

Robert J. O'Neill, *The German Army and the Nazi Party, 1933–1939*, London 1966

Giampaolo Pansa, *L'esercito di Salo nei rapporti riservati della guardie nazionale repubblicana 1943–1944*, Milan 1969

Robert O. Paxton, *Parades and Politics at Vichy: The French Officer Corps under Marshal Pétain*, Princeton, 1966

Dieter Petzina, *Autarkiepolitik im dritten Reich: Der national sozialistisches Vierjahresplan*, Stuttgart 1968

Andrew J. Pierre, *Nuclear Politics: the British experience with an independent strategic force, 1939–1970*, Oxford 1972

L. Pratt, 'The Anglo-American Naval Conversations on the Far East of January 1938', *International Affairs*, 47, 1971

Francesco Pricolo, *La Regia Aeronautica nella secondo guerra mondiale, November 1939–November 1941*, Milan 1971

George Quester, *Deterrence before Hiroshima; the airpower background of modern strategy*, New York 1966

Espagnac du Ravey, *Vingt ans de politique navale, 1919–1939*, Grenoble 1941

Gerhard Ritter, *Carl Goerdeler and the German Resistance Movement*, London 1957, translation of *Karl Goerdeler und die deutsche Wiederstandsbewegung*, Stuttgart 1954

The Sword and the Sceptre, London 1969–73, translation of *Staatskunst und Kriegshandwerk*, 4 vols, Munich 1954–68

Bruce Robertson, *Spitfire: the story of a famous fighter*, Letchworth 1960

I. M. Robertson, *Hitler's Prewar Policy and Military Plans 1933–1939*, London 1963

Giorgio Rochat, *L'Esercito Italiano da Vittorio Veneto a Mussolini (1919–1920)*, Bari 1967

Militari e Politici nella Preparazione della Campagna d'Etiopia: Studio e documenti 1932–1936, Milan 1971

'Mussolini et les forces armées' in *La Guerre en Mediterranée 1939–1945* (Actes du Colloque Internationale), Paris 1971

Hans Roos, 'Die Militärpolitische Lage und Planung Polens genüber Deutschland im 1938' in *Wehwissentschaftliche Rundschau* 7, 1957

R. N. Rosecrancz, *Defence of the Realm: British strategy in the nuclear epoch*, New York 1968

Stephen Roskill, *Naval Policy Between the Wars*, London 1968

Francesco Rossi, *Mussolini e lo Stato Maggiore*, Rome 1951

Vivian Rowe, *The Great Wall of France: the triumph of the Maginot Line*, London 1959

Michael Salewski, *Die deutsche Seekriegsleitung 1935–1941*, Frankfurt 1970

Entwaffnung und Militärkontrolle in Deutschland 1919–1927, Munich 1966

Hilary St George Saunders and Denis Richards, *The Royal Air Force, 1939–1945*, 3 vols, London 1953–4

Admiral B. Schofield, *British Sea Power*, London 1967

Otto Ernst Schüddekopf, *Das Heer und die Republik*, Frankfurt 1955

Hagen Schulze, *Freikorps und Republik 1918–1920*, Boppard am Rhein 1969

Edward A. Shils, *Torment of Secrecy: the background and consequences of American security policies*, Glencoe, Illinois 1956

Helmut Speidel, 'Reichswehr und Rote Armee' in *Vierteljahresheft für Zeitgeschichte*, I, 1953

Umberto Spigo, *Premesse tecniche della disfatta*, Rome 1964

Paul Sterhlin, 'Réalités Stratégiques en 1939', *Revue de la défense nationale*, 28, 1959

R. H. S. Stolffi, 'Equipment for France in 1940', *History*, 55, 1969–70

Mario Tedeschi, *La Guerra dei Generali*, Milan 1968

Telford Taylor, *Sword and Swastika: the Wehrmacht in the Third Reich*, London 1953

Georg Tessin, *Formationsgeschichte der Wehrmacht 1933–1939*, Boppard am Rhein 1959

Georg Thomas, *Geschichte der deutschen Wehr und Rüstungswirtschaft 1918-1943/45*, Boppard am Rhein 1966

Paul Emile Tournoux, *Haute Commandement: Gouvernement et défense des frontières du nord et de l'est, 1919–1939*, Paris 1960

E. S. Turner, *Gallant Gentleman: a portrait of the British officer, 1600–1956*, London 1956

Karl Heinz Völker, *Die deutsche Luftwaffe 1933–1939*, Stuttgart 1967

Thilo Vogelsang (ed.), 'Neue Dokumente zur Geschichte der Reichswehr 1930–1935', *Vierteljahresheft für Zeitgeschichte*, 2, 1954

Reichswehr, Staat und NSDAP, Stuttgart 1962

D. C. Watt, 'The Anglo-German Naval Agreement of 1935', *J. Mod. History* 28, 1956

'Anglo-German Naval Negotiations on the eve of World War II', *J. Royal United Services Institute*, CIII, 1958

'German Military Plans for the Reoccupation of the Rhineland: A Note', *J. Contemporary History*, I, 1966

'German Strategic Planning and Spain, 1938–1939', *Army Quarterly*, LXXX, 1960

'The Rome-Berlin Axis: Myth and Reality', *Review of Politics*, 22, 1961

'Stalin's First Bid for Sea Power', *Proceedings of the US Naval Institute*, 90, 1964

D. C. Watt, *Personalities and Policies: Studies in the formulation of British foreign policy in the twentieth century*, London 1965

Gerhard Wettig, *Entmilitarisierung und Wiederbewaffnung in Deutschland, 1943–55*, München 1967

Sir John W. Wheeler-Bennett, *The Nemesis of Power*, London 1953

Warren E. Williams, 'Para-militarism in inter-state relations', unpublished PhD Thesis, London 1964

R. Wohlfeil and H. Dollinger, *Die deutsche Reichswehr: Zur Geschichte des Hundert-Tausend Mann-Heeres*, Frankfurt 1972

D. Wood and D. Dempster, *The Narrow Margin*, London 1961

Robert J. Young, 'The influence of the military on French foreign policy', unpublished PhD Thesis, London 1969

'Preparations for Defeat: French war doctrine in the inter-war period', *Journal of European Studies*, 2, 1972

Index

Polaris submarine, 150
Pontecorvo, nuclear physicist, passed
'secrets' to Soviet agents, 84
Power relationships, within European states systems, 23-4
Purple Primer, the, British army
manual on armoured warfare, 63

Radar, 82, 92: as major technological
development, 60-61; invention of,
73-4
Raeder, Admiral Erich, Chief of
German naval staff, 109
Rapallo policy, 57, 146-7
Reichenau, General von, 45, 48, 104,
126
Reichstag, growing power of before
1914, 31
Reichswehr, 56-8, 64, 153-5
Remarque, Erich Maria, *Im Westen
nichts neues*, 32
Reynaud, Paul, French Premier in
1940, 138-9
Rhenish separatist movement, spon-
sored by French army, 36
Ribbentrop, Joachim von, 117, 128
Richmond, Admiral Sir Herbert,
British naval theorist, 78
Roosevelt, President Franklin D., 84,
112-14, 149; reluctance to appreciate effects of American policy
regarding Britain's war debts to
America, 113
Rosenberg, Alfred, Nazi 'philo-
sopher', 58
Rotblat, Josef, nuclear physicist, 84
Royal Air Force: formation of, 47;
success against *Luftwaffe*, 68;
adopts Spitfire and Hurricane, 75;
doctrine of defence through counter-bombing, 76-7; control exercised over Royal Navy by, 78;
vision of strategic deterrence, 149;
desire for new long-range bombers,
149
Royal Navy: failure to recognise

long-range naval warfare as victory
development, 77-8; bears brunt of
strategic planning in 1920s; Polaris
missile imposed on, 150
Runstedt, Field Marshal Karl Rudolf
von, 147
Russia *see* Soviet Union
Rutherford, Ernest, 1st Baron,
nuclear physicist, 26, 82

SA, 28-9, 44, 104: suppression of, 48;
purge in leadership of, 93, 104
St Cyr, French military academy, 36,
139
Salisbury Committee, 78
Saló, Republic of, 136, 143
Salomon, Ernest von, *Die Geäch-
teten*, 32
Scapa Flow, mutinies, 29, 46-7
Schacht, Dr Hjalmar, 107, 115; urges
détente with France, 115; resigna-
tion, 115
Schellenberg, Walther, 146
Scheringer trials, 41
Schlabrendorff, Fabian von, 134
Schlesser, Colonel, French military
ideologist, 152
Schlieffen Plan, 85
Schleicher, General von, 41, 44-5,
155; murder of, 48
Schneider-Creusot, French arma-
ments firm, obsolescence of
machine tools in 1930s, 92
Schulenberg, Werner von, 146-7
Schulung, code name, 105
Schumann Plan, rejection of, 151
Schweppenberg, General Geyr von,
German military attaché in Lon-
don, 106
Schwerin, Count von, 29, 128, 134,
153
Scientific world in Britain, willing-
ness to co-operate in official policy,
82
Second World War: confined to
Europe, 11-13; production of four